What Makes a Terrorist

What Makes a Terrorist

Economics and the Roots of Terrorism

Lionel Robbins Lectures

With a new afterword by the author

ALAN B. KRUEGER

PRINCETON UNIVERSITY PRESS

Princeton and Oxford

Copyright © 2007 by Princeton University Press

Published by Princeton University Press, 41 William Street, Princeton, New Jersey 08540

In the United Kingdom: Princeton University Press, 6 Oxford Street, Woodstock, Oxfordshire OX20 1TW

All Rights Reserved

Fourth printing, and first paperback printing, 2008
Paperback ISBN: 978-0-691-13875-6

The Library of Congress has cataloged the cloth edition of this book as follows

Krueger, Alan B.
    What makes a terrorist : economics and the roots of terrorism : Lionel Robbins lectures / Alan B. Krueger.
        p.   cm.
    Book is based on three lectures given by author as part of the distinguished Lionel Robbins memorial lecture series at the London School of Economics and Political Science, February 2006.
    Includes bibliographical references and index.
    ISBN 978-0-691-13438-3 (hardcover : alk. paper)
    1. Terrorism.   2. Terrorism—Economic aspects.   3. Terrorists.   I. Title.
    HV6431.K72   2007
    363.325'11—dc22   2007018413

British Library Cataloging-in-Publication Data is available

This book has been composed in Sabon, Gotham, and Scala Sans by Princeton Editorial Associates Inc., Scottsdale, Arizona

Printed on acid-free paper. ∞

press.princeton.edu

Printed in the United States of America

10 9 8 7 6 5

To the memory of

Pat Tillman,

*whose life exemplified
the courage and dedication
of American heroes
and whose death revealed
their shameful exploitation*

CONTENTS

PREFACE

This book is based on a set of three lectures that I gave as part
of the Lionel Robbins Memorial Lecture Series at the London
School of Economics and Political Science, February 21–23,
2006. That these lectures were delivered on the subject of terrorism is largely a result of the happenstance of world events.
When he initially invited me to speak, on behalf of the selection
committee, in the spring of 2005, Lord Richard Layard strongly suggested that I present the lectures on the economics of education. Although I had done enough research on education to
fill a book, I was at the time most actively engaged in research
on terrorism. My instinct was to present the lectures on the
causes and consequences of terrorism.

We agreed that I would think about the topic. Then, on the
morning of July 7, 2005, England suffered one of the worst
peacetime attacks in its history, when four young men set off
bombs on three underground cars and a bus in central London. Fifty-two people were killed and some seven hundred
were injured. This terrorist attack came on the heels of a dead-
lier one on commuter trains in Madrid on March 11, 2004,
and, of course, the tragic September 11, 2001, terrorist attacks
in the United States. In July 2005 we agreed that there would

be great interest in a set of lectures on the economics of terrorism. Each night the Old Theatre was packed, and the audience asked thoughtful and spirited questions.

The fact that the perpetrators of the July 7 attacks illustrated one of the findings of my research, that terrorists are not necessarily drawn from the ranks of the poor and uneducated —in this case, they were mostly educated, middle-class men from Pakistani and Jamaican families living in Leeds and Aylesbury—made the audience receptive to my lectures. In the lectures, which were originally titled "International Terrorism: Causes and Consequences," I tried to reach beyond anecdotes and individual cases to paint a more complete picture of terrorism. One can always find specific incidents that support one side or another of an argument; the challenge that interested me was to put forth systematic evidence on the causes and effects of terrorism.

There was never any doubt that I would agree to deliver the Robbins Memorial Lectures. The Robbins series is a wonderful institution with which to be associated. Past lecturers have included Rudi Dornbusch, Amartya Sen, Paul Krugman, Peter Temin, Lawrence Summers, Jeff Sachs, Pedro Aspe, Yegor Gaidar, Karl Otto Pohl, William Baumol, Lester Thurow, Robert Barro, Alan Blinder, Daniel Kahneman, Richard Freeman, Robert Mundell, Olivier Blanchard, Richard Layard, Daron Acemoglu, and Andrei Shleifer. Although I never met Lionel Robbins, I have been influenced by his work, and I greatly enjoyed the opportunity to meet his children, who warmly embraced me during my stay in London.

While doing the research summarized in this book, I have received valuable feedback and help from many people. Clara Anderson, Eleanor Choi, Avinash Kishore, Ryan Quillian, and Cathy Rampell provided indispensable research assistance. I am especially indebted to two previous co-authors, David Laitin and Jitka Malečková, who, in addition to giving me sage advice as I revised this book, greatly influenced my thinking and tutored me on international relations and world history. I also thank Alberto Abadie, Claude Berrebi, Martin Feldstein, Jeanne Hull, Christina Paxson, Steve Pischke, Jesse Shapiro, and John Taylor for valuable comments. I am grateful to Lord Richard Layard, Christopher Johnson, and Sir Howard Davies for moderating the three lectures and adding their own useful observations. Last, but certainly not least, Seth Ditchik, Peter Dougherty, Peter Strupp, and their staffs at Princeton University Press and Princeton Editorial Associates deserve credit for expertly and expeditiously converting my lectures into a handsome bound book.

Introduction

IN THE WAKE of the terrorist attacks on September 11, 2001, policy makers, scholars, and ordinary citizens asked a key question: Why did they attack us? What would make someone willing to give up his (or her) life to wreak mass destruction in a foreign land?

In short, what makes a terrorist?

Although the answer to this question is complex and surely varies from case to case, many turned to a simple explanation: economic deprivation and a lack of education cause people to adopt extreme views and turn to terrorism. This explanation appealed to a wide range of people, from President George W. Bush and Prime Minister Tony Blair to religious figures of all faiths to public intellectuals. The alleged connection between poverty, lack of education, political extremism, and terrorism continues to resonate with top government officials, even those who leave office and are no longer obliged to toe the party line. For example, Richard Armitage, the deputy secretary of state from 2001 to 2005, published an op-ed piece in the *New York Times* on Pakistan's problems with terrorism that claimed, "General Musharraf has shown that he understands the seriousness of dealing with the root causes of extremism, making real efforts to improve economic and educational opportunities" (Armitage and Bue, 2006, p. 11).[1]

Within the Muslim community, a distinguished group of thirty-nine imams and ulama (religious leaders and scholars) signed a statement that claimed, "The tragedy of 7th July 2005 demands that all of us, both in public life and in civil and religious society, confront together the problems of Islamophobia, racism, unemployment, economic deprivation and social exclusion—factors that may be alienating some of our children and driving them towards the path of anger and desperation" (Muslim Council of Britain, 2005, p. 2). Rowan Williams, the archbishop of Canterbury, chalked up terrorism to "economic powerlessness" (Williams, 2006). And in his acceptance speech upon being awarded the Nobel Peace Prize in 2006 for his work on micro loans, the economist Muhammad Yunus of Bangladesh said that it was essential to put "resources into improving the lives of the poor people" to end the root cause of terrorism (Yunus, 2006).

Although there is a certain surface appeal to blaming economic circumstances and lack of education for terrorist acts, the evidence is nearly unanimous in rejecting either material deprivation or inadequate education as an important cause of support for terrorism or of participation in terrorist activities. The popular explanations for terrorism—poverty, lack of education, or the catchall "they hate our way of life and freedom" —simply have no systematic empirical basis. These explanations have been embraced almost entirely on faith, not scientific evidence.

---

1. Mr. Armitage later became known for his role in leaking Valerie Plame's identity to Robert Novak. The second lecture describes his handling of the State Department's 2004 terrorism report, *Patterns of Global Terrorism*, which was strewn with errors and subsequently recalled and reissued.

While people who are unemployed or employed in low-paying jobs have a low cost of engaging in political and protest activities and may be angry because of their circumstances, the fact is that they typically do not lash out at the world. Half of the world's population lives on $2.00 a day or less (Chen and Ravallion, 2005). More than one billion people worldwide have a primary school education or less and some 785 million adults are illiterate (Barro and Lee, 2000; Central Intelligence Agency, 2007). If poverty and inadequate education were causes of terrorism, even minor ones, the world would be teeming with terrorists eager to destroy our way of life. Contrary to the popular stereotype, as expressed by Richard Armitage and many others, the uneducated, impoverished masses are particularly *unlikely* to participate in political processes, through either legitimate or illegitimate means.

Instead of being drawn from the ranks of the poor, numerous academic and government studies find that terrorists tend to be drawn from well-educated, middle-class or high-income families. Among those who have seriously and impartially studied the issue, there is not much question that poverty has little to do with terrorism. For example, *The 9/11 Commission Report* was quite clear on the role of economic deprivation in spurring individuals to participate in terrorism: "Terrorism is not caused by poverty" (National Commission on Terrorist Attacks upon the United States, 2004, p. 378). Yet the claim that poverty is the root cause of terrorism continues to be made.

There are many potential explanations for the common misunderstanding that terrorists are motivated to attack us because they are so desperately poor or uneducated that they have nothing to live for, or that they resent the West because it is rich or enjoys certain freedoms. At a theoretical level, economists expect people who have a low opportunity cost of time—that is, a low wage in the legitimate labor market—to turn to crime. But terrorism is different than ordinary property crime.

Most terrorists are not motivated by their own material gain. How could one account for an excess of volunteers for suicide missions if that were the case? Instead terrorists are motivated by political goals that they believe are furthered by their actions. The West is often a target—not because it is rich, but because it is influential and because terrorism has a greater chance of succeeding when it is perpetrated against a democracy than an autocracy.

Rather than street crime, I argue that a better analogy is to voting. Having a high opportunity cost of time—resulting, say, from a high-paying job and a good education—should discourage people from voting, yet it is precisely those with a high opportunity cost of time who tend to vote. Why? Because they care about influencing the outcome and consider themselves sufficiently well informed to want to express their opinions. Terrorists also care about influencing political outcomes. Instead of asking who has a low salary and few opportunities, to understand what makes a terrorist we should ask: Who holds strong political views and is confident enough to try to impose their extremist vision by violent means? Most terrorists are not so desperately poor that they have nothing to live for. Instead they are people who care so deeply and fervently about a cause that they are willing to die for it.

It matters if policy makers and the public have the wrong understanding of what makes people turn to terrorism. For one thing, if we are to craft an effective strategy to combat terrorism, we had better know what is motivating the terrorists. Terrorists are not simply lashing out because they are desperately poor; they are responding to geopolitical issues. Misperceptions of terrorists' motives can inhibit us from addressing the real roots of the problem. Even if policy is off the table—for example, because a government decides it does not want to negotiate over a political issue that is at the root of the grievances motivating a terrorist organization—understanding the causes of terrorism could help prevent countries from pursuing counterproductive courses of action. Curtailing civil liberties, for example, may inspire more people to resort to violent means than are prevented from carrying out terrorist attacks. Understanding the causes of terrorism can also help us to predict how our actions will affect the likelihood of future terrorist attacks. Finally, an accurate understanding of terrorists' motives can help us to put the destructive actions of terrorist attacks behind us, demystify terrorism (and therefore blunt some of the fear of terrorism), and enable society to move on and put the risks of future attacks into perspective.

This book is based on three lectures that I delivered as part of the distinguished Lionel Robbins Memorial Lecture Series at the London School of Economics and Political Science in February 2006. I draw heavily from economics, my own discipline, but also weave in relevant findings from political science, psychology, and sociology. Indeed I first thought of calling this book *Enlisting Social Science in the War on Terrorism*, but I ultimately opted for a simpler title. I strongly believe that a multidisciplinary approach is needed to study adequately the causes and effects of terrorism, especially in light of the failure of basic economic factors like poverty to explain participation in terrorism.

The first lecture examines participation in terrorism at the micro level, the level of the individual. A wide range of data on participants in terrorism is reviewed. Researchers have used ingenious methods to assemble data on terrorists, including scouring the biographies of suicide bombers. The characteristics of those who join terrorist organizations or participate in terrorist acts are compared with those of the relevant population at large. As a group, terrorists are better educated and from wealthier families than the typical person in the same age group in the societies from which they originate. There are, however, occasional exceptions to this pattern. Indeed terrorists are hard to profile because there is no single, unique profile. Terrorist organizations are adept at deploying people who do not fit the profiles authorities are looking for. Nevertheless there is no evidence of a general tendency for impoverished or uneducated people to be more likely to support terrorism or join terrorist organizations than their higher-income, better-educated countrymen.

In addition to examining the characteristics of those who participate in terrorism, the first lecture draws evidence from public opinion polls. Terrorism occurs within a social context. People are encouraged or discouraged to participate in terrorism by friends, family, co-workers, neighbors, and other associates. The evidence from public opinion polls reveals that the best-educated members of society and those in higher-paying occupations are often more radicalized and supportive of terrorism than the most disadvantaged. The illiterate, underemployed population is often unwilling to express an opinion about policy issues, probably because they have more pressing matters on their minds.

The evidence at the individual level should give pause to those who argue that people join terrorist groups because they are impoverished or uneducated. But it does not foreclose the possibility that terrorists are motivated by inadequate or unequal economic opportunities in their own countries. It is possible that members of elites become terrorists because they are outraged by the economic conditions of their fellow countrymen. The second lecture addresses this issue. While it is inherently difficult to determine whether societywide conditions motivate particular individuals, there is again little support for the view that economic circumstances are an important cause of participation in terrorism. A range of socioeconomic indicators—including illiteracy, infant mortality, and gross domestic product per capita—are unrelated to whether people become involved in terrorism. Indeed, if anything, measures of economic deprivation have the opposite effect than the popular stereotype would predict in the country-level analyses: international terrorists are more likely to come from moderate-income countries than poor ones.

One set of factors does consistently raise the likelihood that people from a given country will be ensnared in terrorism, namely, the suppression of civil liberties and political rights, including freedom of the press, the freedom to assemble, and democratic rights. When nonviolent means of protest are curtailed, malcontents appear to be more likely to turn to terrorist tactics. If favorable economic circumstances operate in any way to reduce terrorism, it is by raising the likelihood that a country can sustain civil liberties and political rights. But there are many examples of countries with low living standards that provide their citizens with civil liberties and political rights, and enough examples of rich countries (like Saudi Arabia) that restrict civil liberties and political rights, to make it clear that raising living standards is not by itself sufficient for reducing the risk of terrorism.

Coincidentally the second lecture, which contains a quantitative analysis of the national origins of foreign fighters captured in Iraq, was delivered on February 22, 2006, the day the al-Askari golden mosque in Samarra was bombed, an event considered by many to be a turning point in the Iraq war. In October 2006 the U.S. Central Command prepared a classified briefing on Iraq that was later leaked to the *New York Times*. It contained a color-coded chart titled "Index of Civil Conflict (Assessed)" (Gordon, 2006). On the left of the chart, relative stability and peace in the pre-Samarra days are depicted in soothing shades of green and yellow; on the right, the descent into sectarian violence, ethnic cleansing, and chaos in the days after Samarra is portrayed in increasingly alarming shades of orange and red. Among other things, my analysis reveals the importance of a lack of civil liberties in countries near Iraq in motivating foreigners to join the insurgency. Economic factors were not important in explaining the national origins of the foreign insurgents, but religion was: foreign insurgents were much more likely to come from Muslim countries. The evidence also suggests that the bulk of the Iraqi insurgency, even in the pre-Samarra era, has been drawn from domestic sources.

Terrorists seek to spread fear and thereby disrupt the economy, influence public opinion, and change government policies in their target countries. Do they succeed? The third lecture considers the economic, psychological, and political consequences of terrorism. The lecture also touches on the way the media reports on terrorist attacks, focusing on incentives to sensationalize terrorism, because terrorists rely on media coverage to spread fear and accomplish their ultimate aims.

The economic consequences of terrorism are a matter of much dispute. Some economists argue that terrorism poses a major threat to the economy, while others argue that, in some circumstances, it can in fact lead to stronger economic growth. Consider the views of two prominent economists. In an interview shortly before he died, Milton Friedman asserted that the biggest risk to the world economy was "Islamofascism, with terrorism as its weapon" (Varadarajan, 2007). At the other extreme, Harvard's Robert Barro wrote in *Business Week* that a silver lining of the September 11 attacks was that they would probably end the "near-recession" that the U.S. economy was experiencing by loosening constraints on deficit spending by the government (Barro, 2001).[2]

The third lecture assembles and evaluates available evidence on the economic consequences of terrorist attacks. One conclusion is that terrorists only affect the economy if the public

---

2. According to the National Bureau of Economic Research's Business Cycle Dating Committee, a recession began in March 2001 and ended in November 2001.

lets them, that is, if people and their leaders overreact. The economic consequences of terrorism are inherently tied to its psychological and political consequences, and to media coverage of terrorist attacks because terrorism—as awful and reprehensible as it is—leaves the bulk of the human and physical capital stock intact.

While it is easier to disprove a hypothesis than to prove it, empirical research is rarely persuasive beyond a reasonable doubt in the social sciences. The evidence against material deprivation being a systematic cause of terrorism is stronger at the individual level than at the societal level. It is easier to compare the profiles of terrorists to the population than it is to identify the characteristics of societies that lead a small number of people to turn to terrorism. Even at the individual level, however, some uncertainty remains. While available evidence from a range of settings points to terrorists coming disproportionately from more advantaged backgrounds compared with the population at large, there are some important cases about which little is known, such as the Tamil Tigers of Sri Lanka, and there is conflicting evidence in the case of Northern Ireland.

An even greater barrier to providing persuasive evidence is the paucity of consistent data on terrorist attacks over time at the country level, although the situation is improving now that the National Counterterrorism Center is putting more resources into monitoring terrorist incidents. Researchers have been creative in finding data sources, but the development of an authoritative cross-country database on international terrorist incidents—one that is publicly available, so that researchers can check each others' findings—would lead to improved analysis.

The field of terrorism research is growing rapidly. I have updated the lectures for this book but have otherwise tried to remain faithful to the original lecture format, including presenting an edited version of the question-and-answer sessions that followed the lectures. The book aims to provide an accessible summary and evaluation of the available evidence. Readers need not have a background in statistics to follow the lectures, although I have endeavored to base my conclusions on the best available statistical evidence. Discussions of regression results, standard errors, and multicollinearity are kept to a minimum and typically confined to tables or an appendix, if included at all. References to the underlying research are provided where applicable. Those interested in more details of the statistical analyses are particularly encouraged to read an article I published in the *Journal of Economic Perspectives* with Jitka Malečková and two papers that I co-wrote with David Laitin, a political scientist at Stanford (Krueger and Laitin, 2004b, 2007; Krueger and Malečková, 2003). These articles, along with some additional unpublished material and data used in the book, are available on my web page at www.krueger.princeton.edu.

1

Who Becomes a Terrorist? Characteristics of Individual Participants in Terrorism

FOR THE PAST six years or so I have been studying various aspects of the economics of terrorism. This lecture asks why individuals participate in terrorism: What are their characteristics? Can we infer something about their motivation, the causes behind their participation, from their characteristics and family backgrounds?

I am often asked, "What does this have to do with economics? Why would an economist choose to work on this topic?"

I have two answers, one somewhat flip and the other more serious—although I believe that both are valid. The flip answer is that participation in terrorism is just a special application of the economics of occupational choice. Labor economists are, after all, experts on occupational choice. Some people choose to become doctors or lawyers or economists, and others pursue careers in terrorism. If economics can add something to our understanding of occupational choice in general, perhaps it can be applied to understand participation in terrorism.

The second answer is that, together with Jörn-Steffen Pischke, now at the London School of Economics, I studied the outbreak of hate crimes against foreigners in Germany in the early 1990s. Through this work (Krueger and Pischke, 1997), I became interested in whether economic factors play a role in people's participation in hate crimes and terrorism. The bottom line from the work on hate crimes, which carries over to my research on the economics of terrorism, is that poor economic conditions do not seem to motivate people to participate in terrorist activities. This appears to hold true at both the individual level and the societal level.

Here I address the individual level. In the following lecture I describe research conducted at the country level, and I discuss the characteristics of countries that are either havens for terrorists or targets of terrorists. In the final lecture I consider the economic consequences of terrorism, and you will see that I have a fairly broad definition of economics that reaches into psychology as well as other measures of well-being.

A number of world leaders and prominent thinkers have drawn a connection running from poor economic conditions and lack of education to the outbreak of terrorism. President George W. Bush was initially quite reluctant to make this association after September 11, but eventually—prompted I think by his desire to appear compassionate and by the widespread popular support for the idea—he decided to draw a connection, too. In a major speech he gave in Monterrey, Mexico, on March 22, 2002, for example, President Bush said, "We fight against poverty because hope is an answer to terror" (G. W. Bush, 2002). His wife Laura Bush went further, claiming, "A lasting victory in the war against terror depends on educating the world's children because educated children are much more likely to embrace the values that defeat terror" (L. Bush, 2002). Other world leaders and people responsible for important international institutions made similar comments. For example, James Wolfensohn, when he was president of the World Bank, said, "The war on terrorism will not be won until we have come to grips with the problem of poverty and thus the sources of discontent."

Former British Prime Minister Tony Blair has, on multiple occasions, made a connection between economic conditions and terrorism. On November 12, 2001, he said, "The dragon's teeth of terrorism are planted in the fertile soil of wrongs unrighted, of disputes left to fester for years or even decades, of failed states, of poverty and deprivation" (Blair, 2001). In July 2005, after the bombings of the London transit system, he reiterated this point: "Ultimately what we now know, if we did not before, is that where there is extremism, fanaticism or acute and appalling forms of poverty in one continent, the consequences no longer stay fixed in that continent" (King, 2005). Elie Wiesel observed that "The fanatic has no questions, only answers. Education is the way to eliminate terrorism" (Jai, 2001). Bill Clinton and Al Gore both made comments along these lines, in addition to President Bush, demonstrating that this is a bipartisan issue in the United States (Gore, 2002). Turkish Prime Minister Recep Tayyip Erdogan, King Abdullah of Jordan, terrorism experts like Jessica Stern of the Kennedy School, and many others have claimed that poverty is a cause of terrorism (Stern, 2000; Fendel, 2005).

Yet I hope to persuade you in this lecture and the next one that there is very little support for a connection between poverty and terrorism. In fact, it is remarkable to me that so many prominent, well-intentioned world leaders and scholars would draw this connection without having an empirical basis for it. A wealth of evidence now shows that any effect of education and poverty on terrorism is indirect, complicated, and probably quite weak.

In my collected articles on education, titled *Education Matters* (Krueger 2003b), I emphasize the many benefits of education for individuals and for society in general. My work certainly supports the view that education confers many benefits. I do not, however, think that a reduction in terrorism is one of those benefits. In fact, I believe that merely increasing educational spending and years of schooling without focusing on the content of education may even be counterproductive when it comes to terrorism.

The literature on hate crimes is older and better developed than the literature on terrorism. Therefore I begin by discussing hate crimes and defining terrorism. Next I address how public opinion relates to terrorism. Then I turn to a profile of terrorists and suggest how one should theoretically model participation in terrorism at a conceptual level.

Defining Terrorism

Terrorism is a notoriously difficult concept to define. In fact, if I were to start in this field from scratch, I would avoid the word *terrorism* altogether and use a more neutral term such as *politically motivated violence*. Terrorism is a tactic. Richard Clarke (2004), who served on the U.S. National Security Council, argued that declaring war on terrorism would be like Franklin Roosevelt or Winston Churchill declaring war on U-boats at the beginning of World War II. It is unusual to declare war on a tactic. Moreover, the tactic of terrorism is difficult to define. There are more than a hundred different scholarly definitions of terrorism. At a conference in 2002, foreign ministers from over fifty Islamic states agreed to condemn terrorism but could not agree on a definition of what it was that they had condemned ("Muslim Nations Fail to Define Terrorism," 2002).

When I talk about terrorism I refer to premeditated, politically motivated violence. Furthermore, the form of terrorism that I consider here is perpetrated by substate organizations and individuals with the intent of influencing an audience beyond the immediate victims.[1] In my definition, the goal of

1. This is not meant to imply that state-sponsored terrorism does not exist or is unimportant. Nation-states have engaged in terrorism throughout

terrorism is to spread fear. The immediate victims are not as important as the broader message sent to the public. One of the problems with defining terrorism is that it requires some understanding of the motivation of the terrorists. In that sense, any classification of politically motivated violence must be somewhat subjective. This is an issue with which organizations that try to measure terrorist activity really struggle.

Hate Crimes

I view hate crimes as a close cousin to terrorism. I define hate crimes as crimes involving violent acts against members of religious, racial, or ethnic groups that are motivated by the members' group affiliation, not by their individual characteristics or actions. Sometimes I combine terrorism and hate crimes into a broader category that I call "randomly targeted acts of violence." The individual victims are random, but the group to which they belong is intentionally targeted because terrorists want to send a message or make a statement.

One reason I begin by looking at hate crimes is that they are often more spontaneous or more likely to be carried out by individuals acting on their own accord, whereas terrorist acts are typically filtered or constrained by an organization. For this reason, I believe hate crimes are more likely to represent the pure "supply function" of those willing to carry out these revolting attacks.[2] A consideration of hate crimes allows for a separation between the activities of those carrying out the act itself and the role of the organization as a filter or facilitator.

---

history. But understanding state-sponsored terrorism requires different methods and data.

2. A supply function in economics represents the willingness of someone to offer a service or sell a good under various conditions.

The modern literature on hate crimes began with a remarkable study by Arthur Raper, published in 1933, titled *The Tragedy of Lynching*. Raper assembled data on the number of lynchings each year in the U.S. South and on the price of an acre's yield of cotton. He calculated the correlation coefficient between the two series to the third decimal point. The correlation was −0.532. (Reporting a correlation coefficient to the third decimal place may portray a false sense of precision, but such a computation was probably a major feat in 1933.) Raper looked at these data and determined that there was an inverse relationship. According to his data, when the economy was doing well, as indicated by an increase in the price of cotton, the number of lynchings declined. This finding launched a literature on the so-called deprivation-aggression hypothesis or frustration-aggression hypothesis. A pair of psychologists at Yale, Carl Hovland and Robert Sears, cited Raper's work in 1940 to argue that economic deprivation leads to aggression. They argued that people take out their frustrations on others when economic conditions are poor (Hovland and Sears, 1940). Those studies were the beginning of the U.S. literature on hate crimes and the first that I am aware of to argue that there is a connection between economic conditions and terrorist-like acts.

The problem with this view is that it lacks a strong empirical basis. Green, McFalls, and Smith (2001) published a paper that demolished the alleged correlation between economic conditions and hate crimes in Raper's data. They pointed out that Raper merely discovered two trends that happened to be moving in opposite directions. If you run a multiple regression and control for a time trend, looking at the year-to-year deviations from the ongoing trends, you find no relationship between the number of lynchings and the price of an acre of cotton. Moreover, if you use better measures of economic conditions, like Simon Kuznets's measure of GDP, you also find no relationship. Most importantly, Raper had the misfortune of stopping his analysis in 1929. After 1929, of course, the Great Depression hit. The price of cotton plummeted and economic conditions deteriorated, yet the number of lynchings continued to fall. Extending Raper's series by eight years reveals that the price of cotton crashed but the number of lynchings did not shoot up, as one would have expected if there were a causal deprivation-aggression relationship. Instead, the number of lynchings continued on its downward trend. The correlation disappears altogether when more years of data are added.

Subsequent research has gone further to refute the supposed correlation between hate crimes and economic conditions. Green, Glaser, and Rich (1998) published a study on the occurrence of anti-gay, anti-Semitic, and anti-black hate crimes in New York City using monthly data. They found no relationship between the citywide unemployment rate and the occurrence of these crimes.

A different type of study was carried out by Philip Jefferson and Fred Pryor, economists at Swarthmore. They sought to understand which areas in the United States contain at least one hate group. They found that 10 percent of the 3,100 counties in the United States were home to a hate group in 1997 (Jefferson and Pryor, 1999). Jefferson and Pryor obtained their data from the Southern Poverty Law Center, which reported that the Ku Klux Klan was the most common hate group. The pair of economists used this information to predict the location of hate groups. They investigated whether the existence of hate groups is related to the unemployment rate in the area or to the gap in earnings between blacks and whites. They found no relationship with either economic indicator. Interestingly, however, they did find a positive association between average level of education and the existence of hate groups. Jefferson and Pryor conjectured that hate groups and hate crimes are more likely to occur as a result of a breakdown in law enforcement or as a result of official support for these crimes.

Jörn-Steffen Pischke and I published a similar paper in the *Journal of Human Resources* in 1997 in which we studied the incidence of crimes against foreigners across the 543 counties in Germany (Krueger and Pischke, 1997). We were able to study 1,056 incidents that occurred between January 1992 and June 1993. Most of our information came from news reports on violent crimes against Turks, Vietnamese, Yugoslavs, and other foreigners.[3] The largest numbers of victims were Turks. Figure 1.1 shows the number of crimes against foreigners per 100,000 residents.

One can see right away that the incidence of hate crimes was far higher in the east than in the west. This possibly could be attributed to the fact that economic circumstances in the east were worse than in the west at this time. However, this explanation is unlikely because, within the east or within the west, hate crimes show very little relationship with economic circumstances. For example, in the depressed northwest coast area (circled in the figure), there were few incidents of hate crimes. This is clear from Figure 1.2, which shows the unemployment rate by county. The northwest was an area of relatively high unemployment, yet an area of relatively low ethnic violence. Little correlation between unemployment and ethnic violence can be seen *within* regions.

Our statistical analyses, summarized in Table 1.1, pointed to the same conclusion. In our multivariable analyses we adjusted for the spatial correlation across counties in the outbreak of violence. Ignoring the division between the east and the west, we do

3. A legitimate concern is that events that are reported in the news media are not necessarily representative of the overall pattern. We were able to do some comparisons using official statistics, which for the most part showed similar patterns, but we were unable to obtain official statistics at this low level of geographic detail.

Table 1.1 Regressions for Crimes against Foreigners in All German Counties

| | Means | Regression models[a] | | |
		(1)	(2)	(3)
Unemployment rate	9.5	0.156	–0.124	–0.116
(percent)		(0.054)	(0.085)	(0.077)
West	0.60	—	–3.705	–1.014
			(0.866)	(0.892)
Kilometers to western	43.7	—	—	0.024
border	[East: 110.3]			(0.004)
Percentage foreign	4.4	–0.051	0.031	0.066
		(0.059)	(0.060)	(0.056)
Log population density	5.4	–0.433	–0.407	–0.363
		(0.303)	(0.299)	(0.292)
Moderately urban	0.36	–0.324	–0.186	–0.313
		(0.428)	(0.414)	(0.401)
Moderately rural	0.12	0.728	0.697	0.284
		(0.602)	(0.583)	(0.558)
Rural	0.18	0.514	0.802	0.353
		(0.586)	(0.573)	(0.564)
Kreisstadt (county is	0.22	1.592	1.466	1.388
single city)		(0.688)	(0.680)	(0.664)
Travel time to metropolitan	84.0	—	—	0.011
area (minutes)				(0.004)
Spatial autocorrelation	—	0.385	0.340	0.215
parameter		(0.051)	(0.053)	(0.059)
Number of observations	543	543	543	543

Source: From Krueger and Pischke (1997, Table 3).
Note: Standard errors are in parentheses.
[a]Columns 1–3 present separate maximum likelihood regression estimates in which the dependent variable is the number of violent crimes against foreigners per 100,000 residents in a county.

Figure 1.1 Number of incidents of crime against foreigners per 100,000 residents in Germany, by county, January 1992 to June 1993. The map plots 1,056 incidents of violence against foreigners in 543 counties. The circled area within western Germany has high unemployment yet a low level of crime against foreigners (see text). From Krueger and Pischke (1997).

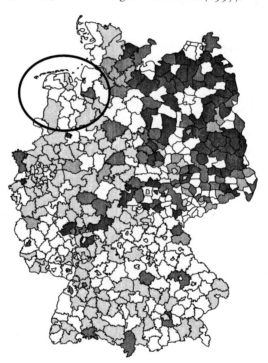

Incidents	Counties
3.75–34	81
1.75–3.75	78
1–1.75	76
0.15–1	92
0.0	216

Figure 1.2 Unemployment rate in Germany, by county, September 1992. From Krueger and Pischke (1997).

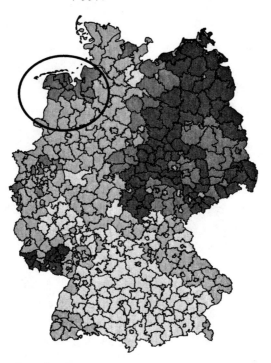

Unemployment
rate   Counties

■ 14.2–19   139
■ 8.2–14.2   133
▨ 5.2–8.2   137
☐ 2.5–5.2   134

find that a higher unemployment rate is associated with more crimes against foreigners, as shown in the column headed (1). However, within the two regions, east and west, we actually find an inverse relationship between the unemployment rate and the incidence of hate crimes, as shown in column (2). Because so many factors besides economic conditions differentiated eastern from western Germany at the time, I think it makes more sense to look at the relationship between unemployment and ethnic violence within the two regions, rather than at how they covary between the two regions. Turning to the other variables, we found that population size mattered, but not population density (people per square kilometer). The number of foreigners in an area or the percentage of the population in an area that was foreign did not matter either (Krueger and Pischke, 1997).

One variable that mattered quite significantly was how far the county was from the west; see column (3). Areas that were farther to the east, within eastern Germany, had higher numbers of crimes against foreigners, other things being equal. It is possible that this pattern was related to economic conditions, in that the farther east you are, the harder it is to commute to the west if you want to get a job there. However, we were able to control for the distance between a county and a city that presented economic opportunities for commuters. We continued to find that the farther east the county was located, the higher was the incidence of hate crimes. In results foreshadowing those of Jefferson and Pryor, we concluded that the farther from the west a county was located (i.e., the farther from more conventional law enforcement practices and greater respect for law), the greater was the breakdown in law enforcement and the higher was the incidence of crime against foreigners after the demise of communism—even though there were relatively few foreigners as one moved farther east. Thus we found no effect of economic conditions on anti-foreigner crimes within a given region. The unemployment rate, the level of wages, wage growth, and average education were all unrelated to the incidence of crimes against foreigners.

Armin Falk and Josef Zweimüller (2005) wrote a paper that found a positive correlation between unemployment and rightwing extremist crime in Germany using state-level data from 1996 to 1999. This paper seems at first to contradict our main finding. However, they studied nonviolent crimes as well as violent crimes, whereas we studied only violent crimes (which are more analogous to terrorist acts). I am not sure if that accounts for the difference. It is worth noting that Falk and Zweimüller found (as we also did) that unemployment and right-wing extremist crime are both more prevalent in eastern Germany, and they hypothesized that there is a causal relationship. However, our results show that, within the two regions, on the county level, there is little correlation between unemployment and violent right-wing extremist crime.

To summarize, across narrow geographic regions or over time, most studies find very little connection between economic circumstances and the incidence of violent hate crimes. Instead, although there are not direct measures of support for law enforcement or respect for the law, the proxies that researchers have available suggest that a breakdown of law enforcement is an important predictor of the incidence of hate crimes.

Public Opinion Surveys

Another important piece of evidence to consider comes from public opinion surveys. Terrorism does not occur in a vacuum. The communities from which terrorists arise are relevant, and the values and views held by different segments of those communities are also relevant. Public opinion polls can help identify those values and views.

The Pew Research Center has conducted the Pew Global Attitudes Project (PGAP), a series of worldwide public opinion surveys. The data I report are from surveys conducted in February 2004 in Jordan, Morocco, Pakistan, and Turkey. The surveys involved about a thousand people in each of those countries (Pew Global Attitudes Project, 2004).

One of the questions asked was, "What about suicide bombing carried out against Americans and other Westerners in Iraq? Do you personally believe that this is justifiable or not justifiable?" In Figure 1.3 I report the percentage of respondents who said that suicide bombing was justifiable, broken down by the respondents' education level for each of the four countries.[4] The level of education ranges from no formal education—which in some of the countries, such as Pakistan, is the case for a very large group—to a university education. The scales of these charts are important. In Jordan, positive responses to this question ranged from about 62 percent to over 70 percent, depending on the respondents' education level. In Turkey, the country for which the number of university-educated respondents was greatest, the scale goes up only to about 34 percent saying that these attacks are justified. In Pakistan the scale depicted in the graph ranges from 35 percent up to 60 percent. The range of the y-axis was set to be the same (25 percentage points) in all these graphs, so the differences in the heights of the bars are comparable. As these graphs demonstrate, people with a higher level of education are in general *more* likely to say that suicide attacks against Americans and Westerners in Iraq are justified. In Jordan and Pakistan the pattern is not monotonic but seems to dip down at the university level; but this evidence certainly does not indicate that the uneducated or those who are poorly educated were more supportive of such bombings.

Another important finding from these data is that those who have a lower level of education are more likely to answer

4. I thank Nicole Speulda of the Pew Research Center for providing the tabulations underlying these figures and for answering many questions.

Figure 1.3 "What about suicide bombing carried out against Americans and other Westerners in Iraq? Do you personally believe that this is justifiable or not justifiable?" Results by education level. Based on Pew Global Attitudes Project (2004).

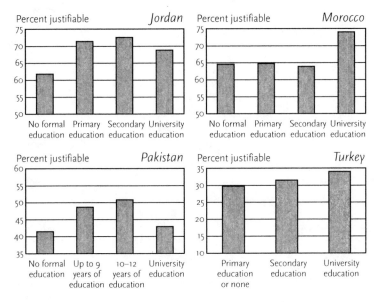

"no opinion" when they are asked questions like these. This could lead to an understatement of the percentage who say suicide bombing is justified in the lower educated groups, but the pattern is still evident in the difference between those who say it is justified and those who say it is not, and the excess number of "no opinions" should also affect the percentage who say it is not justified. Additional questions that ask specifically about suicide attacks against Israel, and then about suicide attacks in general or attacks intended to protect Islam, generally show the same pattern.

I have also broken this pattern down by income level (Figure 1.4), but the income data are not particularly good in this survey. I have income data for Jordan, Pakistan, and Turkey, although for Pakistan the data are reported in very broad

Figure 1.4 "What about suicide bombing carried out against Americans and other Westerners in Iraq? Do you personally believe that this is justifiable or not justifiable?" Results by income level. Based on Pew Global Attitudes Project (2004).

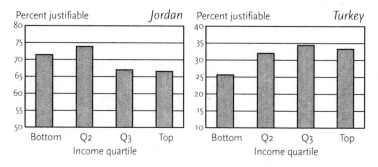

ranges that are not very informative and hence are not presented here. There is no indication that at higher levels of income people are less likely to say that suicide bombing attacks are justified. In Turkey respondents are more likely to say that such attacks are justified if they have a higher level of income, and in Jordan and Pakistan there is a weak relationship between income and stated belief that suicide bombing is justified.[5]

Palestinian Public Opinion Surveys

The Palestinian Center for Policy and Survey Research (PCPSR), a professional survey group headquartered in Ramallah, collects public opinion data on attitudes toward violence against Israel in the West Bank and Gaza Strip. They have conducted a series of surveys over several years. I rely on data from December 2001, just before Israel's major incursion into the West Bank. The surveys were conducted in face-to-face interviews of over 1,300 people age 18 and over (Palestinian Center for Policy and Survey Research, 2001). The PCPSR was very kind to provide

5. See Malečková (2006) for related evidence from PGAP surveys in five Muslim countries in 2002.

Table 1.2 "In your opinion, are there any circumstances under which you would justify the use of terrorism to achieve political goals?"

| | Education level of respondent (percent) | | | | |
	Illiterate	*Elementary school*	*Middle school*	*High school*	*Greater than high school*
Yes or definitely yes	32.3	37.5	36.9	39.4	36.4
No or definitely no	45.3	53.4	55.3	51.4	56.7
No opinion	22.4	9.2	7.8	9.2	6.9

Source: Tabulations provided by the Palestinian Center for Policy and Survey Research. Survey of 1,357 Palestinians, age 18 and older, conducted December 19–24, 2001, in the West Bank and Gaza Strip.

me with tabulations from their data in the midst of an extraordinarily difficult period in Israeli-Palestinian relations.

Question 16 on the survey asked, "In your opinion, are there any circumstances under which you would justify the use of terrorism to achieve political goals?" In Table 1.2 I have broken down the responses by education level. There exists no clear pattern of support for terrorism as a means to achieve political goals by education level. About a third of the public in all education groups said "yes" or "definitely yes." Closer to half said "no" or "definitely no." The illiterate were much more likely to say "no opinion," which is consistent with the results of the Pew surveys mentioned earlier: those with a low level of education are less likely to express an opinion.

It is significant that terrorism here was not defined. The respondent was free to define terrorism any way he or she liked. These surveys, however, show that the definition the respondents implicitly used is different from that which would commonly be used in the West. For example, in the survey used in Table 1.2, which was conducted a few months after September 11, 2001, a majority, 53 percent, said they did not consider the attacks on the World Trade Center to be terrorism. They did say that they believed the rest of the world would consider the attacks to be terrorism. Eighty-two percent said they did not think that the June 2001 suicide bombing of the Dolphinarium Nightclub in Tel Aviv, Israel, which killed twenty-one youths, was an act of terrorism. Again, however, they seemed to recognize that the rest of the world would view this attack differently.

Question 17 asked, "Do you believe that armed attacks against Israeli civilians inside Israel so far have achieved Palestinian rights in a way that negotiations could not?" Remember, this question was asked in 2001, when relatively little had been achieved in securing Palestinian rights. But over 60 percent of respondents across almost all groups replied "yes" (Table 1.3). There seems to be no obvious pattern by education here. One of the things I take away from these data is that the Palestinian population has long believed that the armed attacks against Israeli civilians were efficacious and helped to advance their cause. Interestingly there was little change in the responses to this question (or similar ones) from 2001 to 2005, although beginning in 2006 confidence in the view that armed confrontations had helped achieve Palestinian rights began to wane. In the December 2006 survey, 49 percent of Palestinians agreed that "armed confrontations so far had helped achieve Palestinian national and political rights in ways that negotiations could not achieve," while 49 percent disagreed (Palestinian Center for Policy and Survey Research, 2006). This shift in public opinion, if it continues, could possibly signal a greater willingness on the part of Palestinians to negotiate with Israel.

The next question in the 2001 survey addressed people's attitudes toward armed attacks on Israeli targets, with the option to say "strongly support," "support," "oppose," "strongly oppose," or "no opinion." Here support is stronger among those who have a higher level of education (Table 1.4). And

Table 1.3 "Do you believe that armed attacks against Israeli civilians inside Israel so far have achieved Palestinian rights in a way that negotiations could not?"

	Education level of respondent (percent)				
	Illiterate	*Elementary school*	*Middle school*	*High school*	*Greater than high school*
Yes or definitely yes	56.8	63.3	64.8	63.3	59.9
No or definitely no	36.4	33.1	32.9	34.2	37.4
No opinion	6.8	3.6	2.3	2.4	2.8

Source: Tabulations provided by the Palestinian Center for Policy and Survey Research. Survey of 1,357 Palestinians, age 18 and older, conducted December 19–24, 2001, in the West Bank and Gaza Strip.

Table 1.4 "Concerning armed attacks against Israeli targets, I:"

	Education level of respondent (percent)				
	Illiterate	*Elementary school*	*Middle school*	*High school*	*Greater than high school*
Support or strongly support	72.2	80.5	82.1	86.1	81.5
Oppose or strongly oppose	25.9	17.5	15.3	12.0	13.9
Have no opinion	1.9	2.0	2.6	1.9	4.6

Source: Tabulations provided by the Palestinian Center for Policy and Survey Research. Survey of 1,357 Palestinians, age 18 and older, conducted December 19–24, 2001, in the West Bank and Gaza Strip.

there are few "no opinion" responses when the question is asked in this way. When asked about terrorism in general, about a third of respondents say that they think it can be justified. Asked more specifically about attacks on Israeli targets, closer to 80 percent say that armed attacks against Israeli targets are justified. The illiterate are actually less supportive than those who are better educated, even though 72 percent of the illiterates said that they support or strongly support these attacks. Forty-six percent more illiterates responded "support or strongly support" than "oppose or strongly oppose," compared to a 68 percent difference among those with education greater than a high school degree. These findings indicate that the expressed strength of support for terrorism seems to be rising with education level among Palestinians.

In September 2004 the same question was asked again in a slightly more specific manner. The questions distinguished between attacks within Israel and in the West Bank. The responses showed much stronger support for attacks in the West Bank, with 90 percent of respondents showing support, than inside Israel, with 54 percent supporting the attacks. The data have not yet been broken down by education level. Support for attacks inside Israel fell sharply in the 2005 polls, but rebounded to the 2004 and earlier level in 2006.

I was able to have the responses to the 2001 question on support for attacks against Israeli targets broken down by occupation. These surveys did not include income data, but occupation can be used as an indicator of socioeconomic status. These data, summarized in Table 1.5, reveal several notable patterns. First, the least supportive group is the unemployed. Seventy-four percent of the unemployed said they support or strongly support armed attacks against Israeli targets. Compare that to merchants and professionals, 87 percent of whom supported the attacks. The greatest degree of expressed support (90 percent) came from students, a finding that is not

Table 1.5 "Concerning armed attacks against Israeli targets, I:"

	Occupation of respondent (percent)				
	Student	*Laborer*	*Housewife*	*Merchant or professional*	*Unemployed*
Support or strongly support	89.7	80.8	82.0	86.7	73.9
Oppose or strongly oppose	9.4	16.0	15.7	10.0	23.9
Have no opinion	0.9	3.1	2.3	3.3	2.2

Source: Tabulations provided by the Palestinian Center for Policy and Survey Research. Survey of 1,318 Palestinians, age 18 and older, conducted December 19–24, 2001, in the West Bank and Gaza Strip.

surprising, considering that students are often the most radicalized segment in a society. Bear in mind also that these students are age 18 and over, and so are primarily college students. Housewives responded similarly to the overall population, with 82 percent indicating their support.

The level of support for these attacks in the general population was distressingly high. Of course, this apparent support is something that people are saying in response to a questionnaire or to an interviewer; it is not clear that these answers represent their heartfelt feelings or would motivate their behavior. Nevertheless, based on socioeconomic status as measured by occupation or education, it is not the least-well-off members of the society who express the greatest degree of support for attacks against Israelis. Instead, it is the better-educated and those who are in higher-status professions who tend to show more support.

It turns out that related findings have been around for a long time. Daniel Lerner, a professor at MIT at the time, published a book in 1958 called *The Passing of Traditional Society* in which he collected and analyzed data on extremism in six Middle Eastern countries. He tabulated responses to questions concerning support for extremism. Lerner concluded that "the data obviate the conventional assumption that the extremists are simply the have-nots. Poverty prevails only among the apolitical masses" (Lerner, 1958, p. 368). I believe that this is a generally robust finding that transcends time and space. The most notable possible exception that I have found seems to be Northern Ireland, which I will discuss further later in this lecture.

Finally, the PCPSR survey included questions about whether people were optimistic for the future. Respondents were asked, "Do you believe the economy is improving? Do you think that the situation is better over the last three years than it was before then or do you think the situation is worse?" Responses to these questions suggest that, just before the outbreak of the second intifada, the population believed that the economic situation was improving (Figure 1.5). This belief was consistent with the falling unemployment rate at the time. The second intifada did not appear to be caused by dashed expectations for future economic conditions, as optimism was still rising when it began in September 2000 (Palestinian Center for Policy and Survey Research, 2001).

From Polls to Participation

It is a long way from expressing support in a public opinion poll to actually participating in acts of terrorism. I turn now to the evidence on participation, beginning with a review of some anecdotal evidence. Nasra Hassan, a U.N. relief worker in the West Bank and Gaza Strip, published a remarkable article in the *New Yorker* in which she described interviews with 250 militants and

Figure 1.5 Responses to Palestinian Center for Policy and Survey Research survey questions regarding Palestinians' optimism for the future.

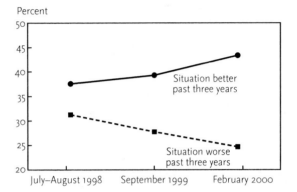

their associates who were involved in the Palestinian cause in the late 1990s. She concluded that "none of them were uneducated, desperately poor, simple minded or depressed. Many were middle class and, unless they were fugitives, held paying jobs. Two were the sons of millionaires." One Hamas leader told her, "Our biggest problem is the hordes of young men who beat on our doors, clamoring to be sent on suicide missions. It is difficult to select only a few" (Hassan, 2001, p. 36).

This remark highlights the fact that the organizations have screened those whom they send on terrorist missions, selecting based on some criterion. In all probability, they are looking for those who are most likely to succeed—a logical criterion, because if a failed mission is traced back to the leaders, the consequences can be extremely costly. Ariel Merari, a psychologist at Tel Aviv University, has studied terrorists who were involved in failed terrorist attacks and has concluded that they were unlikely to be psychologically abnormal. They did not seem to be particularly depressed, for example (Merari, 2005).

Claude Berrebi, now of the RAND Corporation's Institute for Civil Justice, wrote his dissertation at Princeton on the

Figure 1.6 Comparison of Palestinian suicide bombers to Palestinian population, West Bank and Gaza Strip. Sample size is 48 for suicide bombers and 18,803 for population. Suicide bombers were from Hamas and the Palestinian Islamic Jihad. From Berrebi (2004).

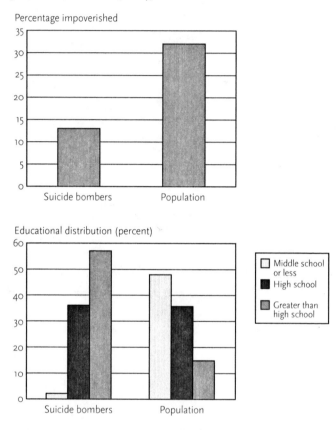

characteristics of those from the West Bank and Gaza Strip who were involved in terrorist activities. Instead of studying exclusively those involved in terrorism, he compared suicide bombers and other militants to the whole male population age 16 to 50. Figure 1.6 shows the percentage of suicide bombers who came from impoverished families versus the percentage of the population as a whole living in poverty. The suicide bombers were less than half as likely to come from families that were below the poverty line (Berrebi, 2004).

In addition, almost 60 percent of the suicide bombers had more than a high school degree, compared to less than 15 percent of the general population (Berrebi, 2004). These numbers are not terribly surprising because both Hamas and the Palestinian Islamic Jihad, from which these data were drawn, recruited mainly on college campuses. Those who attend college tend to be the children of middle-class and wealthy families.

Biographical Information

I performed a similar analysis on members of Hezbollah, a multifaceted organization that includes a political wing, a social wing, and a resistance wing. The group was founded in the early 1980s to resist the Israeli occupation of Lebanon. It is believed to have been responsible for suicide truck bomb attacks against the U.S. embassy and Marine barracks in Lebanon as well as French paratroopers. The U.S. State Department and the British Home Secretary have declared Hezbollah to be a terrorist organization, but, during the period I studied it, it might more appropriately have been termed a resistance organization. I was able to obtain information on the biographies of 129 deceased shahids (martyrs) who had been honored in Hezbollah's newsletter, Al-Ahd. These biographies were translated by Eli Hurvitz at Tel Aviv University (Hurvitz, 1998). I turned his translations into a dataset and then combined it with data on the Lebanese population from the 1996 Lebanese Ministry of Social Affairs Housing Survey of 120,000 people aged 15 to 38. The data are described in greater detail in Krueger and Malečková (2003).

The data, to be sure, have serious limitations. Not all members of the Hezbollah sample were engaged in terrorism, raising questions as to whether the sample is representative. In addition, this dataset was made up of only the deceased, and therefore it may have included a disproportionate number of foot soldiers, who had a higher mortality rate. (On the other hand, it was estimated that about a third of the organization had been killed in action, so our data represent a reasonably large fraction.) The data are noisy and the sample is small, but obtaining high quality data on terrorists obviously is not easy. The population sample also has some problems. It does not align perfectly with the years covered by the Hezbollah sample. The differing definitions of poverty in the two datasets could also pose a problem. Most importantly, I do not have data on religion. Therefore in my analysis I narrow the sample to the south of Lebanon, to the more heavily Shiite regions where Hezbollah recruited. In my statistical analysis, I also take into account the fact that the Hezbollah sample is over represented compared with its share in the population because of the way the samples were constructed.

Table 1.6 reports some summary statistics. Members of Hezbollah actually have a slightly lower poverty rate than the Lebanese population: 28 percent versus 33 percent. The deceased members of Hezbollah were better educated: 47 percent had a secondary or higher education versus 38 percent of the Lebanese population. Members of Hezbollah also seemed to be younger, even though I limited the sample from Lebanon to ages 15 to 38, to correspond to the age range of the deceased members of Hezbollah in my sample.

I used these data to estimate a logistic equation to model participation in Hezbollah, controlling for several factors simultaneously. I found that members of Hezbollah were better educated than the relevant segment of the Lebanese population, less likely to come from impoverished families, and younger (Table 1.7). The results we saw in the simple summary statistics seemed to hold up in more sophisticated statistical analyses (Krueger and Malečková, 2003).

Table 1.6 Comparison of Deceased Hezbollah Militants to Lebanese Population, Ages 15 to 38

	Deceased Hezbollah militants (%)	Lebanese population (%)
Impoverished background	28	33
Education level		
Illiterate	0	6
Read and write	22	7
Primary school	17	23
Preparatory school	14	26
Secondary school	33	23
University	13	14
Postgraduate studies	1	1
Age		
15–17	2	15
18–20	41	14
21–25	42	23
26–30	10	20
31–38	5	28
Region of residence		
Beirut	42	13
Mount Lebanon	0	36
Bekaa	26	13
Nabatieh	2	6
South	30	10
North	0	22

Note: The p-values for tests of the hypothesis that the percentages are equal for the Hezbollah militants and Lebanese population are .489 for impoverished background, .000 for education level, .000 for age, and .000 for region.

Table 1.7 Logistic Estimates of Participation in Hezbollah

| | All of Lebanon | | | | Heavily Shiite areas | |
| | Unweighted estimates | | Weighted estimates | | Weighted estimates | |
	(1)	(2)	(3)	(4)	(5)	(6)
Intercept	-4.886	-5.910	-3.805	-4.826	-4.658	-5.009
	(0.365)	(0.391)	(0.230)	(0.256)	(0.232)	(0.261)
Attended secondary school or	0.281	0.171	0.282	0.171	0.220	0.279
higher (1 = yes)	(0.191)	(0.193)	(0.159)	(0.165)	(0.159)	(0.167)
Poverty (1 = yes)	-0.335	-0.167	-0.335	-0.168	-0.467	-0.500
	(0.221)	(0.223)	(0.158)	(0.163)	(0.159)	(0.166)
Age	-0.083	-0.083	-0.083	-0.084	-0.083	-0.082
	(0.015)	(0.015)	(0.008)	(0.008)	(0.008)	(0.008)
Beirut (1 = yes)	—	2.199	—	2.200	—	0.168
		(0.219)		(0.209)		(0.222)
South Lebanon (1 = yes)	—	2.187	—	2.188	—	1.091
		(0.232)		(0.222)		(0.221)
Pseudo-R^2	0.020	0.091	0.024	0.08	0.021	0.033
Sample size	120,925	120,925	120,925	120,925	34,826	34,826

Notes: Standard errors in parentheses. Dependent variable is 1 if individual is a deceased Hezbollah militant and 0 otherwise. Weights used in columns 3–6 are the estimated relative share of Hezbollah militants in the population to their share in the sample and the relative share of Lebanese household survey respondents in the sample to their share in the population.

I also studied the membership of an Israeli terrorist organization called Gush Emunim, which means "block of the faithful." This was a fanatical religious organization that was active in the early 1980s. In 1980 it attempted unsuccessfully to blow up the Dome of the Rock mosque. The group was also responsible for the murders of several West Bank mayors. A Gush Emunim member, Haggai Segal, wrote a book titled *Dear Brothers* in which he summarized the backgrounds of several participants (Segal, 1988). I used this account, among other sources, to obtain information on twenty-seven members of the organization. A summary of their backgrounds is in Table 1.8. Gush Emunim included engineers, teachers, a computer programmer, a geographer, and a combat pilot; its members appeared to be drawn from the higher-socioeconomic-status occupations.

Previous Literature on Participation in Terrorism

The descriptions in Table 1.8 are representative of the type of evidence available in the preexisting literature on participation in terrorism. Much of the literature relies on biographies typically culled from newspapers, which might be more inclined to profile those in leadership positions. The literature does not systematically compare the participants in terrorism to the population at large, but it nonetheless tends to find overwhelming evidence that participants are skewed toward higher socioeconomic-status occupations. This is also the case with al-Qaeda. Marc Sageman, a forensic psychiatrist and former Central Intelligence Agency (CIA) case officer, has written a book titled *Understanding Terror Networks,* based on unclassified data. Among other things, he studied the education and occupational backgrounds of members of al-Qaeda. He did not compare al-Qaeda members to the populations from which they were drawn, but he nevertheless found that a

Table 1.8 Characteristics of Israeli Jewish Underground Terrorists in the Early 1980s

Name	Year of birth	Occupation	Underground activity
Katriel Avinoam	1965+	Army officer	Related to the conspiracy to blow up the Dome of the Rock mosque, 1980.
Dan Be'eri	1945	Established an elementary school in Kiryat Arba; founder of the Barkai educational method	Related to the conspiracy to blow up the Dome of the Rock mosque, 1980 (left the group in 1982).
Haim Ben-David	1952	Geography and history expert	Related to the conspiracy to blow up the Dome of the Rock mosque, 1980, and participated in the attack on the National Guidance Committee, 1980.
Yeshua Ben-Shushan	1946	Not available	Instigated the conspiracy to blow up the Dome of the Rock mosque, 1980.
Yehuda Cohen	Not available	Yeshiva student	Carried out the reconnaissance on the Temple Mount.
Yossi Edri	Not available	Electrician	Participated in the acquisition of the clocks used in the attempt to blow up Arab buses, April 27, 1984.

Yehuda Etzion	1951	Farmer and writer	Prime mover in the Dome of the Rock conspiracy and key figure in the attacks on the West Bank mayors.
Yitzhak Ganiram (Akaleh)	1945	Teacher and special education instructor for learning-disabled youth	Participated in the attacks on the West Bank mayors; offered limited assistance in the Dome of the Rock conspiracy. Let the perpetrators of the Islamic College killings use his car.
Aaron (Roni) Gilo	Not available	Army captain	Not a member of the underground, but used his military position to aid those involved in the attacks on the West Bank mayors.
Benzion (Bentz) Heineman	1936	Religious scholar and farmer	Helped carry out the technical preparations for several underground operations.
Boaz Heineman	Not available	Owner of a farm and carpentry shop	Prepared explosives for the underground.
Yaakov Heineman	1948	Air force combat pilot and farmer	Played a limited role in the conspiracy to blow up the Dome of the Rock mosque, 1980.
Shlomo Liviatan	Not available	Army officer	Played a limited role in the attack on the West Bank mayors.

(continued)

Table 1.8 Continued

Name	Year of birth	Occupation	Underground activity
Menachem Livni	1950	Engineer	Participated in planning all operations associated with the underground.
Uri Meier	Not available	Farmer	Participated in the aborted attack on Bethlehem's Dr. Ahmed Natshe.
Natan Natanson	1957	Not available	Involved in the attacks on the West Bank mayors.
Menachem Neuberger	1965	Yeshiva student	Participated in gathering intelligence for the attacks on the West Bank mayors.
Barak Nir	Not available	Teacher	Participated in the attack on the Islamic College and in the attempt to sabotage the Arab buses.
Shaul Nir	1954	Engineer	Involved in the Islamic College killings and initiated the attempt to blow up Arab buses.
Yitzchak Novik	1948	Chemist, farmer	Participated in the attacks on the West Bank mayors.

Gilad Peli	Not available	Farmer and Israel geography expert	Participated in the attacks on the West Bank mayors; participated in the Dome of the Rock conspiracy.
Era Rappaport	1948	Not available	Participated in the attacks on the West Bank mayors.
Haggai Segal	1957	Reporter and university student	Participated in the attacks on the West Bank mayors.
Uzi Sharbaf	1960	Physical education teacher	Involved in the Islamic College killings; initiated the attempt to blow up Arab buses.
Yosef Tzuria	1959	Computer programmer	Related to the conspiracy to blow up the Dome of the Rock mosque.
Noam Yinon	1957	Farmer	Convicted of supplying explosives to Menachem Livni and Shaul Nir.
Moshe Zar	1937	Land dealer	Driver in the attacks on the West Bank mayors.

Sources: Segal (1988); Black and Morris (1991); Friedman (1992); and Neff (1999).

high percentage of them were college educated (close to 35 percent) and drawn from skilled professions (almost 45 percent) (Sageman, 2004).

I think there is general agreement in the literature that most terrorist organizations are composed of people drawn from the elites. The U.S. Library of Congress produced a summary report for an advisory group to the CIA, "The Sociology and Psychology of Terrorism: Who Becomes a Terrorist and Why?" which also reached this conclusion (Hudson, 1999). I first learned of this report after September 11, when it was cited by the Bush administration to intimate that the Clinton administration should have been better prepared for a terrorist attack involving an airplane. It was a low-level report prepared for a low-level committee. I read the report very closely and—although I found it absolutely fascinating—I could not find a mention of terrorists using an airplane in an attack. So I did a control-F search, and, sure enough, buried in the report was a mention that al-Qaeda could retaliate for the U.S. cruise missile attack on their training facilities in 1998 by crashing an airplane packed with explosives into the Pentagon, CIA headquarters, or the White House. I give the report credit for recognizing that terrorist organizations were becoming more sophisticated, were composed of well-educated individuals, and were becoming able to carry out more sophisticated acts of terrorism. And I give the Bush administration credit for subsequently finding the report's speculation about the possible use of an airplane in a terrorist attack.

The (Probable) Puzzle of Northern Ireland

The Library of Congress report included a fascinating discussion of the literature on participation in terrorism. The report recognized that many terrorist cadres have predominantly middle-class or even upper-class backgrounds and are well educated, with many members having university degrees. However, it also pointed out that Irish groups, such as the Irish Republican Army (IRA), are poorly educated. Christina Paxson of Princeton's Woodrow Wilson School studied a survey question asked in Ulster in 1968, just before inflation, high unemployment, emigration, and poor economic governance began to take their toll on the Irish economy. Respondents were asked whether they agreed or disagreed that it would be justifiable to take any measures necessary to end partition and bring Ulster into the republic. Twelve percent of Catholics agreed and 81 percent disagreed. Paxson found that support for taking any measure was lower among those with higher education: an extra year of schooling was associated with a 3.2-percentage-point reduction in the probability of agreeing that any measure would be justifiable (Paxson, 2002). Her results also appeared to show that income was unrelated to whether people agreed or disagreed.

In terms of education, the results of the Irish opinion poll are different from those of the Middle Eastern polls I described earlier. In addition, the regions in Northern Ireland that were more likely to support the IRA and more likely to participate in terrorism seemed to be those that were more economically depressed. However, a time series analysis by Thompson (1989) of the relationship between the unemployment rate and the number of fatalities in the conflict in Northern Ireland from 1922 through 1985 found no association. Therefore, there appears to be a discrepancy between the regional data and the time series data. Nevertheless, I believe that there are enough indicators that members of the IRA were disproportionately working class—even within regions and within ethnic or religious groups in their communities—to make relevant the question of why Northern Ireland appears to be so different.

It is a question to which I do not have a definitive answer, although I do have some conjectures. One possible explanation for why the IRA was drawn disproportionately from the working class is that those who were destined for the middle class but were particularly unhappy emigrated to the United States. Another possibility, which is mentioned in the literature from time to time, is that discrimination against Catholics prevented a middle or upper class from developing in Northern Ireland. I find this explanation difficult to accept because, in other situations where discrimination exists, participants in terrorist organizations still tend to be from relatively well-off, better-educated backgrounds. The final hypothesis is that terrorism in Northern Ireland may be more like guerrilla warfare or civil war than the activities of a small terrorist organization. There is a body of literature on who participates in civil war and whether economic circumstances affect the outbreak of civil war; it finds that economically depressed areas are more likely to undergo a civil war.

Know Thy Enemy

Terrorists themselves do not tend to highlight economic factors in their own rhetoric. For example, in a tape that was aired on the Arabic television channel al-Jazeera, a man believed to be Mohammad Sidique Khan, the leader of the July 7, 2005, London bombings, said, "I and thousands like me are forsaking everything for what we believe. Our driving motivation doesn't come from tangible commodities that this world has to offer" ("London Bomber Video Aired on TV," 2005). In this statement he explicitly acknowledges that his and his fellow terrorists' actions are not driven by their economic circumstances, although one should be aware that his cell represents only a very small sample. It could also be noted that the July 7 London attackers do not appear to be particularly impoverished. Khan goes on in this tape to describe his motivation as a form of retaliation for the West's activities.

We see here a pattern that is observed time and again: although those who have lower socioeconomic status or lower education might have a lower opportunity cost of participating in terrorism, lower-income people prioritize material gains over ideological goals, perhaps out of necessity. One conclusion I draw is that the well-off and better educated are drawn to extreme positions, as we have seen in the public opinion polls. Those who are less educated are more likely to say that they have no opinion. Those who are better educated are also more likely to vote. People who are better educated and earn a higher income have a higher opportunity cost of voting. Yet that does not discourage them from voting, probably because they believe in the process and because it is less costly for them to become informed and to form opinions on issues that make them want to vote. People who have a higher level of education find it easier and less costly to acquire information. They also seem to have greater confidence in their opinions, and that could lead to extremism.

One could argue that economic conditions still matter for the supply side, that, even though terrorists are not drawn disproportionately from the ranks of the illiterate and poor, they are nonetheless motivated by inequality in their societies or by the poverty of their countrymen. I call this Robin Hood terrorism. The next lecture will, however, cast some doubts on the validity of this theory of terrorism.

The size of the movement may also matter for supply-side determinants of terrorism. If terrorist organizations are small, they tend to be composed of the elites who care deeply about the cause. They are the first ones to join. For the movement to grow past a certain point, it must recruit a wider pool of members because the truly committed are already involved. Beyond a certain size, the additional recruits tend to be motivated more by pay and less by ideology; these tend to be people of lower socioeconomic status. For a civil war to occur, a terrorist or insurgent group must reach a certain scale. In this event, the organization is composed not only of those who care deeply about the cause but also mercenaries.

On the demand side, terrorist organizations prefer to have highly skilled individuals carry out terrorist acts, given the high costs of failure. There is more skill involved in implementing terrorist attacks than is commonly appreciated. The two London bombings in July provide a case study of a well-executed versus a poorly executed terrorist plot. The second attack appeared to be a failure because it was carried out by people who were less sophisticated and less well educated than those who orchestrated the first attack. In their recent paper, "Attack Assignments in Terror Organizations and the Productivity of Suicide Bombers," Efrain Benmelech and Claude Berrebi (2007, p. 1) assert that "more able suicide bombers should be assigned in equilibrium to targets that are associated with greater rewards." They find reasonably supportive evidence for this view in their analysis of both failed and successful terrorist attacks in Israel.[6] When it comes to international terrorism, a terrorist must go unnoticed in a foreign society. It is perfectly logical that those whom the organizations select for important and international missions will tend to be better educated and more likely to come from higher-socioeconomic-status backgrounds.

The Market for Martyrs

For the most part, terrorists are *not* people who have nothing to live for. On the contrary, they are people who believe in something so strongly that they are willing to die for it. I think

---

6. Perhaps relatedly, Diego Gambetta and Steffen Hertog (2006) find that engineers are overrepresented in violent Islamist groups.

of terrorism as a market, with a supply side and a demand side.[7] Individuals, either in small groups or on their own, supply their services to terrorist organizations. Terrorist organizations recruit, train, and deploy terrorists.

On the supply side, recognition of opportunity costs and of the economics of crime and of suicide should indicate that people of low market opportunities will become involved. In other domains of life, it is those with few opportunities who are more likely to commit crime and resort to suicide. However, the opportunity cost is outweighed by other factors when it comes to the supply of terrorists. I do not think economic circumstances are irrelevant, but that they are dominated by other forces, such as a commitment to the goals of the terrorist organization. As I emphasized earlier, political involvement requires some understanding of the issues, which is a less costly endeavor for those who are better educated.

On the demand side, the organizations want to succeed, so they select more able participants. They also do not want to be predictable, so they might adopt something of a randomized strategy. The groups that demand the services of terrorists do so to respond to political grievances, and they are often quite strategic in their choice of methods, targets, and timing.

One of the conclusions from Iannaccone's (2003) work, which is supported by my own research, is that it is very difficult to effect change on the supply side. People who are willing to sacrifice themselves for a cause have diverse motivations. If we address one motivation and thus reduce one source on the supply side (such as by reducing poverty), there remain other motivations that will incite other people to terror. Supply is fairly elastic in that sense. Terrorist groups seem to be capable

---

7. See Laurence Iannaccone's (2003) paper "The Market for Martyrs" for more discussion along these lines.

of substituting people from different backgrounds to carry out terrorist attacks. That suggests to me that it makes sense to focus on the demand side, such as by degrading terrorist organizations' financial and technical capabilities, and by vigorously protecting and promoting peaceful means of protest, so there is less demand for pursuing grievances through terrorist tactics. Policies intended to dampen the flow of people willing to join terrorist organizations, by contrast, strike me as unlikely to succeed.

Conclusion

Finally we must ask the question, "Why is the popular stereotype that poverty and inadequate education cause terrorism so popular?" The public seems to buy into this myth. Their belief that terrorists act because they are desperate and uneducated is sustained—as the quotations at the beginning of this lecture indicated—by the frequent pronouncements of world leaders, who should know better.

I have a few conjectures as to why there is so much popular support for this view. One reason is that we tend to see the world through materialistic Western eyes, viewing economic circumstances as powerful motivators for belief and action. In addition, assuming that those who attack us do so because they are desperate or because they hate our way of life provides a reassuringly simple answer to a disturbingly complex question. Many world leaders exploit the overly simple logic that poverty causes terrorism in order to further their own interests, to press for more international aid for their countries or institutions, or to deflect attention from policies that provoke grievances and extremism.

The discussion becomes much more complicated, however, if we hypothesize that terrorists are motivated by some grievance concerning American activity in the Middle East, such as the presence of American troops in the Persian Gulf and American support of autocratic regimes friendly to the United States. If we acknowledge that terrorists are motivated by geopolitical grievances instead of desperation, then we have to confront their grievances. And we may not want to confront their grievances. The West may be well justified in dismissing either particular grievances or inappropriate ways of expressing them. However, I believe it is wrong for the West to fail to appreciate that our policies can lead to negative or even violent consequences. One of the great contributions of economics is the idea of a response function. If one party does something, the other party may be expected to respond. If Continental Airlines drops the price of its Newark-to-London flight, for example, British Air is likely to respond in kind. It is important to acknowledge that this process operates in foreign policy as well, and to try to predict these responses while formulating policy.

I must acknowledge that, although lack of education and income are not important root causes of terrorism, they can be part of the solution. I am pessimistic that they will ever constitute an important part of the solution, but it is nevertheless important to improve education and reduce poverty around the world. Nothing I have said about terrorism in this lecture should change that view. If education is to be part of the solution, I believe it is important that we concentrate on the content of education. I do not think that merely increasing years of schooling with the same curriculum that exists now will improve the situation. In fact, as we have seen, such an approach could lead to heightened extremism. Research is necessary to learn what subject areas and educational materials lead to greater tolerance and respect for nonviolent forms of protest rather than self-righteousness and extremism.

I fear that drawing a false connection between poverty and terrorism can be dangerous. If we, like President Bush in his Monterrey speech, seek to couch support for international aid as part of the war against terrorism, support for such aid might wane as the fear of terrorism recedes. This occurred, to some extent, after the end of the cold war, with disastrous consequences for Africa. I think that the West has a moral obligation to support economic development around the world. Incorrectly linking poverty to terrorism can be counterproductive to our efforts to reduce the former even as we confront the latter.

2

**Where Does Terror Emerge?
Economic and Political
Conditions and Terrorism**

IN THIS LECTURE I consider the macro evidence on terrorism, at the society or country level. I begin by discussing the data that the U.S. government collects on international terrorism. In the course of my research I quickly discovered that there is a burning need for better data on the frequency and lethality of terrorist activity, underscored by the entertaining but ultimately sad anecdote I include here, recounting how the government bungled the assembly of its most authoritative data on terrorism. I nevertheless analyze the imperfect data that are available and conclude with a summary of some new evidence on foreign insurgents in Iraq.

The U.S. Government's
(Flawed) Evidence on Terrorism

The U.S. government should place greater priority on assembling high-quality data on the occurrence of terrorist attacks. For years, the government appears to have hardly considered reporting to the citizenry whether our dollars are well spent, whether we are making progress in combating terrorism, or whether we may actually be hurting our cause.

Until recently, the most authoritative unclassified data on terrorism available in the United States were from a report titled *Patterns of Global Terrorism,* which was prepared by the State Department under a mandate from Congress. Under United States Code Title 22, Section 2656(f), "The Secretary of State shall . . . report for each country: acts of international terrorism, activities during the preceding year of any terrorist group, and any umbrella group under which such terrorist group falls, any terrorist group known to be financed by these countries." The *Patterns* report specifies the following definition of terrorism: "premeditated politically motivated violence, perpetrated against non-combatant targets by sub-national groups or clandestine agents, usually intended to influence an audience. The term 'international terrorism' means terrorism involving citizens or the territory of more than one country" (United States Department of State, 2004).

Interestingly, although the State Department report claims that its definition of terrorism is taken directly from the United States Code, the actual definition in the code does not include the phrase "intended to influence an audience." However, I believe this phrase is a valid component of the definition and narrows the focus to a more relevant range of event types. For instance, many political assassinations or genocides—as horrible as they are—would not be included under this definition, as they are targeted more specifically at individuals or populations and are not intended to send a wider message to a general audience. As I mentioned in the first lecture, while I do not deny the existence of state terrorism, in these lectures I focus on terrorist acts carried out by substate organizations or individuals.

The State Department amended its definition of noncombatants to include, in addition to civilians, military personnel who at the time of an incident are unarmed or are not on duty.

The government also considers terrorism to include attacks on military installations or on armed military personnel when a state of military hostilities does not exist at the particular site. Appendix A to the *Patterns of Global Terrorism* report provides a list of every significant terrorist attack in the preceding calendar year. This list includes information on where the attacks took place, which organizations were responsible, the countries of origin of the perpetrators, the nationalities of those affected, and other details. Importantly, Appendix A allows us to verify that the attacks took place and to collect additional information about them. I analyzed the reports for the years 1997–2002 in the paper that I published with Jitka Malečková in the *Journal of Economic Perspectives*, and I extended the data through 2003 to illustrate those findings here (Krueger and Malečková, 2003).

The text of the report has beautiful charts which list, for each year, the total number of terrorist attacks, including the ones that presumably are considered insignificant. I was browsing through the report for the year 2003, which was released on April 29, 2004, when I noticed a disconnect (which seemed to have been exacerbated in this year, but which was present in the previous few years as well). The glossy graphs in the body of the report show the number of terrorist attacks declining from 426 in 2000 to 190 in 2003 (Figure 2.1). However, the number of significant attacks listed in the appendix is actually rising. In the report that was released on April 29, 2004, the number of significant terrorist attacks was at its highest level since the reports began to be issued in 1982. Yet when the report was released, the State Department claimed that the number of attacks was at its lowest level since they had started collecting such data, and high-ranking State Department officials cited this as proof that the United States is prevailing in the war against terrorism (United States Department of State, 2004).

Figure 2.1 Total international terrorist attacks, 1982–2003. From United States Department of State (2004, p. 176), uncorrected version.

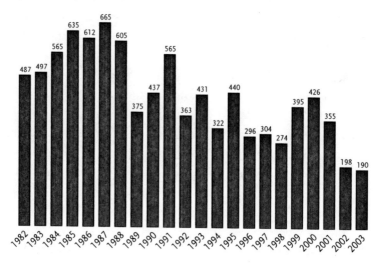

The report for 2003 contained many anomalies. For example, Appendix A is supposed to cover the entire calendar year, but the last event listed occurred on November 11. This would make sense if no terrorist attacks occurred after November 11, but, in fact, on November 15 there were deadly attacks in Turkey on two Jewish synagogues, the British consulate, and a British bank. A few days after that there was a major terrorist bombing in Saudi Arabia. These attacks were well publicized. When I came across these discrepancies, I called the State Department to ask what was going on. Perhaps there had been a printing error through which these significant attacks had been included in the figures but simply omitted from the appendix. I left several messages, but I never received a complete explanation.

In response to this incident, David Laitin and I wrote an op-ed piece, published in the *Washington Post* on May 17, 2004, in which we accused the State Department of manipulating the data. That charge may have been somewhat over the top, as we subsequently learned that the problems with the report were due more to incompetence than manipulation, although officials were quick to claim credit for the apparent success in reducing terrorism. When we went through the report, we discovered that the number of significant terrorist attacks had increased from 124 in 2001 to 169 in 2003, even using the data that ended with November 11 and excluded subsequent attacks. That number, 169, was the highest number of significant attacks since the data were first collected (Krueger and Laitin, 2004a).

After our op-ed article on this saga came out, I expected that we would receive an immediate response from the State Department and that other journalists would follow up on this breaking news. But for three weeks absolutely nothing happened. It was disappointing to me that, although terrorism was such an important issue in the U.S. presidential campaign at the time, so little attention was being paid to the inaccuracy of the government's key report on terrorism. On June 10, Richard Boucher, the State Department spokesman, held a press conference announcing the discovery of errors in the report. He announced that the department would issue a corrected version and that the corrections could fill eight pages. The number of fatalities had reportedly been underestimated by 50 percent (Boucher, 2004). He released the following statement, which I thought was somewhat ironic: "The claims we made were based on the facts we had at the time. The facts turned out to be wrong" (Boucher, 2004). This is almost the same language that had been used to explain the administration's mistaken belief that Iraq possessed weapons of mass destruction. Shortly after Mr.

Boucher made this comment, on June 13, Secretary of State Colin Powell went on *Meet the Press*, a political talk show hosted by Tim Russert. Here is an excerpt from that interview:

RUSSERT: Turn to this report on global terrorism, your credibility being called into question. This is your deputy secretary of state, Richard Armitage, in April [cut to Richard Armitage]: "Indeed, you will find in these pages clear evidence that we are prevailing in the fight." In the fight on terrorism. And the report says this, "There were 190 acts of international terrorism in 2003, a slight decrease from the 198 attacks that occurred in 2002, a drop-off of 45 percent from the level in 2001, 346 attacks. The figures in 2003 represent the lowest annual total of international terrorist attacks since 1969." And then two professors from Princeton and Stanford, they took a look at this and they concluded this: "Yet a careful review of the report and underlying data supports the opposite conclusion. The number of significant terrorist acts increased from 124 in '01 to 169 in '03, a 36 percent [increase]. Even using the State Department's official standards, the only verifiable information in the annual reports indicates that the number of terrorist events has risen each year since 2001. In 2003 it reached its highest level in more than 20 years." Henry Waxman, the Democratic congressman from California, said that you are manipulating data for political purposes.

POWELL: Well, we're not. The data that is in our report is incorrect. If you read the narrative of the report, it makes it clear that the war on terror is a difficult one and that we're pursuing it with all of the means at our disposal. But something happened in the data collection and we're getting to the bottom of it. Teams have been working for the last several days and all weekend long. I'll be having a meeting in the department tomorrow with CIA, other contributing agencies, the Terrorist Threat Information [*sic*]

Center and my own staff to find out how these numbers got into the report. Some cut-off dates were shifted from the way it was done in the past. There's nothing political about it. It was a data collection and reporting error. And we'll get to the bottom of it. We'll issue a corrected report and I've talked to Congressman Waxman.

RUSSERT: Was it CIA data?

POWELL: It's a combination of data that flows in and some of it is CIA. The Terrorist Threat Information [*sic*] Center compiles data, provides it to us. But when you look at it in hindsight now, and you look at the analysis given to me by Congressman Waxman and these two congressmen [*sic*], all sorts of alarm bells should have gone off. All sorts of, as I say to my staff, circuit breakers should have dropped when we saw this data, and they did not. But I don't think there was anything political or policy driven about it. It was just data that was incorrect or wasn't properly measured compared to the way it was measured in previous years. And so what we have to do is normalize the data [for] this past year, 2003, in the same way that [we] normalized data in previous years. And we will be putting out that corrected information as fast as we can.

RUSSERT: But it is embarrassing.

POWELL: Very embarrassing. I'm not a happy camper over this. We were wrong.

After Secretary Powell's appearance on *Meet the Press*, the issue attracted quite a bit more attention. Many people learned about it from watching *The Daily Show*, whose host, Jon Stewart, presented a humorous but pointed critique of the situation. Here is an excerpt:

ANNOUNCER: June 14th, 2004. From Comedy Central's World News headquarters in New York, this is *The Daily Show* with Jon Stewart.

STEWART: Let's begin tonight with some good news on the war on terror. Two months ago, the State Department released its survey of worldwide terrorist acts in 2003, and it turns out the number of such acts was at its lowest level since 1969. At the time Deputy Secretary of State Richard Armitage drew the only logical conclusion: "You will find in these pages clear evidence that we are prevailing in the fight."

You see that, people? Stop focusing on events outside in the world and start looking at these pages. You'll find that if you look at the pages, we're doing quite well. Counterterrorism coordinator Cofer Black, do we have the terrorists on the ropes? [Cut to Cofer Black.] "They are truly under catastrophic stress. They're very defensive." Booyah! In your face, bin Laden! We are taking you down!

Wait. I'm sorry, I'm being told that's all completely wrong. I'm sorry. Yes, as it turns out, the government now acknowledges that the terrorism report was badly flawed and grossly undercounted the number of attacks last year, which in reality was among the bloodiest years ever for terrorism. Uh, oops. Among the report's omissions, three huge bombings, one in Saudi Arabia and two in Turkey, which weren't included because, this is true, they took place in November, after the report apparently needed to go to the printers. Apparently our government is run by the same people who put out your high school yearbook.

The report is so strewn with mistakes, a State Department official says the corrections may fill eight pages. California Congressman Henry Waxman, who condemned the report when it was released, has now stepped up his criticism. [Cut to Henry Waxman.] "The report was based on inaccurate information and they drew political conclusions that were self-serving for the administration." You know, they've kind of been doing that for a while now. It's getting ridiculous. Boy, who's the poor sucker who's got to get out there and defend this one? [Cut to Colin Powell and Tim Russert.] "But it is embarrassing." "I'm not a happy camper." You know what he said? Tim Russert says, it is embarrassing, and Colin Powell says, it is embarrassing and—you may have missed the quote—he said, "I'm not a happy camper."

And you know, ever since this year began, it seems like Colin Powell has had a very poor camp experience. I'd be very surprised to see him come back next summer to this camp. But Powell insists there was no evil intention. "There was no attempt to mislead or cook the books in any way. So far it appears to be honest administrative error." Honest error. *Eight* pages of corrections. The first page or two? Honest errors. Third page, uh, perhaps a questionable half-truth. By page six, you're [expletive] lying. The State Department has announced it will soon release a revised version of the report.

While humorous, this clip is not entirely accurate. Jon Stewart and a State Department spokesman both erroneously claimed that the report's list of terrorist attacks ended on November 11 because the report had to go to the printers. In fact, the errors were due mostly to the low priority that the State Department assigned to the report, meaning that the numbers were not adequately checked. Colin Powell clarified the contents and production of the report to the public as well as to Congressman Waxman's staff. The State Department requested that the Central Intelligence Agency produce data on the number of significant terrorist attacks and the total number of attacks each year. Then the State Department wrote a narrative that was notably independent of the numbers. It is amazing to hear Colin Powell say that the narrative was fine, although the numbers must be changed. Even though some statistics were reported in the narrative of the report, it was written almost without reference to any data or to the findings from the data in the report.

Contrary to what might be considered logical to an economist, the State Department does not appear to use data for objective analysis, but rather solely for public relations and public diplomacy. In his 2003 State of the Union address, President Bush announced with great fanfare the creation of the Terrorist Threat Integration Center (TTIC), a new agency to integrate all of the government's information on terrorism (Bush, 2003).[1] I suspect that the CIA decided to give TTIC all the work that the CIA did not want to do. In addition to this problem, the person who had been responsible for running the computer program that was compiling these data left the CIA at this time and was replaced by an outside contractor. This was not an example of government efficiency in action.

The *Patterns* report contains shockingly little information about how the data were assembled. It says that the government's Incident Review Panel reviews each terrorist attack and determines whether it was significant. However, it fails to specify the criteria for determining significance, the source of the panel's information, or the membership of the panel. We were able to uncover much of that information. For example, we learned that the panel was composed of people who indeed seemed well qualified. However, they rotated so quickly on and off the panel that there was little institutional memory from one meeting to the next.

In an attempt to be constructive, David Laitin and I wrote a piece for *Foreign Affairs* to which the journal gave the brilliant title "Misunderestimating Terrorism." In this article, we suggested that the State Department try to learn from economic statistics. There have been attempts in U.S. history, particularly by President Richard Nixon, to manipulate economic sta-

---

1. Colin Powell, in his June 13, 2004, appearance on *Meet the Press*, had referred to this organization as the Terrorist Threat Information Center.

tistics. In fact, President Nixon ordered that certain federal employees, who he said were misrepresenting data, be transferred from the Bureau of Labor Statistics—when, in fact, he was the one misrepresenting the numbers. After that, procedures were developed and adopted to restrict the ability of political officials, including the president, to comment on the data before they had been presented and interpreted by career staff. We made a series of recommendations for improving the terrorism data in our article; for example, that there be a clear and consistent definition of terrorism, that the data be verifiable, and that career employees with some knowledge of statistics prepare and release the report (Krueger and Laitin, 2004b).

The glossy graphs in the body of the *Patterns* report that show terrorism falling to its lowest level ever are not verifiable. We subsequently discovered that the reason for the sharp downward trend in those graphs was that there had been a large number of attacks on oil pipelines in Colombia that were probably carried out by an oil pipeline repair company to generate more business for itself. When it was discovered that these events did not represent terrorism, they were precipitously dropped, without any explanation. Knowing this background, it becomes clear that these charts are not very informative. But this is not readily apparent because no verifiable information was provided.

My colleague at Princeton, Paul Krugman, wrote a piece in the *New York Times* about this incident after the *Meet the Press* broadcast. He told me that he suspected there was evil intent behind the report's inaccuracies (Krugman, 2004). I responded that I believed it was simple incompetence. If you were going to manipulate the data, you would fill it out so that the chronology actually reached the end of the year. As it is, the errors in the report are quite transparent because it just stops on November 11. Undercounting by 50 percent the number of fatalities was really a page from the Keystone Kops, not Machiavelli. The mistakes were, I believe, "merely" the result of incompetence. Paul wrote this up in the *New York Times* and referred to me as "a forgiving soul" because I was willing to give the government the benefit of the doubt. He also pointed out that, had the mistakes gone in the other direction, they very likely would have been caught. Had the mistakes shown that 2003 had a much higher level of terrorist incidents than previous years (which it actually did), then the responsible agencies would certainly have double-checked the numbers.

In the piece that David Laitin and I wrote for *Foreign Affairs*, we called this problem "asymmetric vetting," meaning that the Bush administration would have vetted the numbers more carefully if they had not supported the position that it wanted to take. We recommended that career professionals be the ones to release the data, not the deputy secretary of state (who, incidentally, was later revealed to be the first source of the Valerie Plame leak).

We also discovered that the State Department is the only cabinet-level department within the U.S. government that does not have a statistical agency. The Department of Education has a statistical agency, the Department of Labor has one, the Department of Commerce has two, the Department of Agriculture has a very well-funded statistical agency—but not the State Department. When the State Department releases numbers, there is no one who is able to check whether there has been a statistically significant change, so the department does not know if the trends it is reporting could have occurred by chance. It is ironic that the State Department has become so averse to statistics, for the first secretary of state, Thomas Jefferson, was a huge fan of statistics. We suggested that the State Department form a statistical agency.

Some of the decisions underlying the State Department data seem inconsistent. An example is events in Chechnya, which are sometimes considered international terrorist attacks and sometimes domestic ones. But there was no way to reconstruct the reason for the variation.

When we made our recommendations, I sent a copy of the preprint to Secretary of State Powell, but I did not receive an acknowledgment. However, the inspector general of the State Department subsequently issued a report on this incident, in which he made many recommendations echoing our own (Krongard, 2004). He did not propose creation of a statistical agency, but he did suggest that the department hire someone with training in statistics to work on the report. In response to the concern about transparency, the inspector general proposed that minutes be kept of the meetings at which the report was assembled, so that one could reconstruct how decisions were made.

Colin Powell did not return to the Bush administration in its second term. Condoleezza Rice became secretary of state. She cut the statistics from the *Patterns* report and renamed it. The level of terrorist activity for 2004 and 2005 was very high, and the State Department decided that it should not be responsible for releasing these numbers. The data are now compiled and released by the National Counterterrorism Center (NCTC), the successor to the Terrorist Threat Integration Center, which in turn was closed down.

So far the NCTC has been evenhanded in releasing the data, and more explicit than its predecessors in describing what it does. They actually asked me for a copy of the Jon Stewart tape to show their analysts what might happen if they slipped up. I have some optimism that the situation may get better, but I think we still have a long way to go before terrorism statistics will deserve to be accorded the same credibility as economic statistics—or even earned run averages in baseball.

Validity of the Data

The State Department issued corrected statistics and, using this new chronology, I extended the dataset from 1997 to 2003. I readily acknowledge that these data have serious problems, only some of which, as I detail below, can be addressed. Nonetheless, for each terrorist event, I identified the home country of the perpetrators and the target country and linked them to information pertaining to both the home and target countries' gross domestic product (GDP) per capita, political rights and civil rights, religious affiliation, and population size. I have compiled, for each possible pair of countries, information on the number of terrorist attacks perpetrated by people from country A against people in country B. I have used a series of statistical models to estimate the relative influence of each factor. The data cover 956 terrorist events from 1997 to 2003.

Here I describe the data in greater detail and present some of the more important findings. I also cite some additional evidence on suicide attacks, including both international and domestic events, based on data from Pape (2003) and the International Policy Institute for Counterterrorism.

There are some issues with the data as we have coded them. For example, embassies are a frequent target. We coded the country where the embassy was located as the place of the attack, but we coded the target as the country whose embassy it was. Another unusual situation is posed by the 280 terrorist attacks that occurred in India during this time (the largest group of attacks), most of which occurred in Kashmir. The State Department records these incidents in an unusual way. Presumably, the department believes that the attacks are carried out by Pakistanis or other foreigners, even though the descriptions in the chronology in *Patterns of Global Terrorism* make them sound as if they were domestic because no foreign nation is mentioned. The second largest number of attacks occurred in

Colombia, and the terrorist nature of these attacks is sometimes questionable. Some of these events represent oil pipeline bombings that were possibly perpetrated by the pipeline repair company, and there are also some instances of kidnapping for ransom, which I might define as crime rather than terrorism. In view of these ambiguities, Colombia was excluded from much of our analysis. The State Department also has difficulty categorizing terrorism in Israel, because the West Bank and Gaza Strip, over most of this period, were not independent entities; they were under Israeli control. Therefore, the department treats most attacks in Israel as domestic terrorism. The data do show a large number of events in Israel, but these are instances in which an American or other foreigner was injured or killed in an attack. Since these incidents are problematic, we dropped them from our dataset later on as well.

There are a number of other datasets on international terrorism, each with its own particular flaws. One of these is the ITERATE data, which were collected by Todd Sandler of the University of Southern California and other colleagues (Mickolus et al., 2006). We compared our data to the ITERATE data, which measured the number of international terrorist attacks *occurring in each country.* The ITERATE dataset includes about 18 percent more terrorist events than our data, suggesting that it may be more comprehensive or that it may include some domestic terrorist attacks. Across countries, our data have a reasonably high correlation with the ITERATE data, .57 or .52, depending on whether our data are tabulated at the level of the country of origin of the perpetrators or the country where the event occurred (Table 2.1).

In our data, we defined the target as the nationality of the people who were most affected by an attack, or that accounted for the largest proportion of those injured. If, for example, a café was blown up and seven Israelis and two Americans were killed, we would code Israelis as the target. If the target was the

Table 2.1 Correlations between Place-Based ITERATE Data and Data Derived from U.S. State Department Reports

	Origin	Place	Primary target
All countries	.57	.52	.23
Excluding India	.89	.90	.41
Number of countries	138	139	136

Notes: In all cases, the ITERATE data are measured at the level of the country where the event occurred. The State Department data were measured at the level of the country of origin of the perpetrators, the country where the event occurred (place), or the country that was the target of the attack.

American Colony Hotel and all the people there were Americans, then we would code Americans as the target. Of course there is some ambiguity in coding the target of specific attacks, and the correlation with the ITERATE data is notably lower at the target level (only .23). Interestingly, if we exclude India, which is an outlier in the State Department data, the correlation rises considerably, up to about .90 at the level of the country of origin or the place where the event occurred, and .41 at the level of the target. These correlations suggest that, with the exception of their results for India, the two datasets are pointing in the same direction.

Table 2.2 shows country-by-country data on the number of attacks, and the number of attacks per million people in the country, based on our coding of the State Department data. India is a clear outlier in terms of the number of attacks, but not on a per capita basis, where it is only slightly above the worldwide figure of 0.16 events per million people. The West Bank and Gaza Strip stand out—as do Sierra Leone, Angola, Bahrain, Yemen, and Colombia—as the highest-ranked countries of origin in terms of international terrorist attacks per capita.

Table 2.2 Number and Frequency of Significant International Terrorist Attacks based on U.S. State Department Chronologies, 1997–2003

Country	Number of events	Events per million population
Azerbaijan	1	0.13
Belgium	1	0.10
Eritrea	1	0.26
Germany	1	0.01
Guinea	1	0.14
Kenya	1	0.03
Nicaragua	1	0.21
Senegal	1	0.11
Thailand	1	0.02
Tunisia	1	0.11
United Arab Emirates	1	0.37
Zambia	1	0.10
Bahrain	2	3.11
Bangladesh	2	0.02
Chad	2	0.27
Cuba	2	0.18
El Salvador	2	0.33
Liberia	2	0.68
Macedonia	2	0.99
Morocco	2	0.07
Myanmar	2	0.04
Tanzania	2	0.06
Uzbekistan	2	0.08
Chile	3	0.20
Democratic Republic of Congo	3	0.06
Egypt	3	0.05
France	3	0.05
Kuwait	3	1.61
Peru	3	0.12
Venezuela	3	0.13
Bosnia	4	1.06
Cambodia	4	0.35

(continued)

Table 2.2 Continued

Country	Number of events	Events per million population
Israel	4	0.67
South Africa	4	0.10
Sudan	4	0.13
United Kingdom	4	0.07
Ecuador	5	0.41
Iran	5	0.08
Jordan	6	1.31
Lebanon	6	1.43
Ethiopia	7	0.11
Italy	7	0.12
Rwanda	7	0.86
Spain	7	0.18
Sri Lanka	7	0.37
Somalia	8	0.98
Yugoslavia	8	0.75
Georgia	9	1.65
Burundi	10	1.53
Uganda	10	0.48
Tajikistan	11	1.80
Indonesia	13	0.06
Algeria	14	0.47
Russia	15	0.10
Greece	16	1.52
Saudi Arabia	17	0.88
Afghanistan	18	0.72
Philippines	20	0.27
Sierra Leone	21	4.35
Iraq	26	1.17
Nigeria	26	0.21
Pakistan	26	0.20
Turkey	32	0.50
Angola	41	3.31
West Bank and Gaza Strip	46	16.84
Yemen	49	2.95
Colombia	104	2.55
India	280	0.29

Characteristics of Victims and Perpetrators

Interestingly, 88 percent of the time, terrorist attacks occur in the perpetrators' country of origin. This finding implies that most international terrorism is in fact *local*. Most of the terrorist attacks in this dataset were carried out by residents of a country on property belonging to a foreign country, such as a McDonald's restaurant, or on foreign nationals who happened to be in the perpetrators' home country. Sometimes foreigners were the main target, and sometimes their deaths or injuries were strictly collateral.

In almost 90 percent of cases, the way we have coded the data, the origin of the perpetrators and the place where the attack occurred are the same. A typical international terrorist attack is thus not like those on September 11, when people from foreign countries came to the United States to commit an attack. That kind of incident is quite rare. A more typical scenario is the kidnapping and murder in Pakistan of the *Wall Street Journal* reporter Daniel Pearl, by a group believed to be affiliated with al-Qaeda.

In about two-thirds of the cases, it was suspected that a specific terrorist organization was involved. In the remaining third, although attacks may have been orchestrated by organizations, it was not clear who those organizations were. In 91 percent of the cases the attacks were carried out by multiple perpetrators. My co-author David Laitin, who is an expert on conflict, made a judgment as to whether the perpetrators and the victims were of the same religion or a different religion. Sixty-two percent of the time there was a difference in religion between the victims and the perpetrators (Krueger and Laitin, 2007). In comparison, there is a 77 percent chance that two randomly selected people on earth will be of different religions. So the 62 percent likelihood that perpetrators and victims of terrorism will be of different religions is not very different from random selection.

As I mentioned earlier, however, most terrorism is local, with the terrorists and a majority of their victims often from the same country, and perhaps a few unlucky foreigners among the victims. Within a given country, the average probability for two randomly selected people to be of different religions is 27 percent (Krueger and Laitin, 2007). This means that the probability is much higher than random chance of finding a difference in religion between the perpetrators and victims of terrorist attacks.

Interestingly, for suicide attacks, 90 percent of the time the victims and the perpetrators are of a different religion. Something about suicide attacks seems to be more closely connected with religious differences.

About 4 percent of the attacks in the State Department's data are on embassies. Twelve percent of the attacks targeted the United States. Seven percent were on international organizations, so—although many people were shocked when the United Nations was targeted in Iraq—it is in fact not uncommon for the United Nations, the Red Cross, or other international organizations to be targeted. Just 5 percent of the attacks were suicide bombings.

Characteristics of Countries of Origin of Terrorists and Their Victims

Table 2.3 breaks down terrorist attacks by the origin or target country and shows rates per million population for various groups of countries. The first set of rows reports results by different quartiles of GDP. Separate figures are shown for suicide attacks. The number in brackets for each grouping is the p-value, which evaluates whether there is a systematic pattern in the data. If the p-value is low, then the pattern across groups of countries probably did not occur by chance. If the p-value is high, the possibility of chance determining the observed differ-

Table 2.3 Terrorist Attacks per Million Population (of Origin or Target Country) by Country Characteristics

Country characteristic	All events		Suicide attacks	
	Origin	*Target*	*Origin*	*Target*
GDP per capita				
Quartile 1 (poorest)	0.37	0.11	0.00	0.00
Quartile 2	0.18	0.07	0.10	0.10
Quartile 3	0.17	0.30	0.19	0.11
Quartile 4 (richest)	0.34	0.47	0.35	0.38
	($p = 0.45$)	($p = 0.00$)	($p = 0.01$)	($p = 0.01$)
GDP growth				
Under median	0.31	0.12	0.01	0.00
Above median	0.23	0.30	0.27	0.24
	($p = 0.44$)	($p = 0.01$)	($p = 0.01$)	($p = 0.00$)
Illiteracy rate				
Under median	0.27	0.26	0.22	0.23
Above median	0.18	0.19	0.11	0.07
	($p = 0.40$)	($p = 0.01$)	($p = 0.61$)	($p = 0.26$)
Civil liberties				
Low	0.42	0.19	0.12	0.07
Medium	0.27	0.38	0.31	0.33
High	0.02	0.12	0.00	0.00
	($p = 0.00$)	($p = 0.00$)	($p = 0.77$)	($p = 0.00$)
Political rights				
Low	0.39	0.11	0.11	0.07
Medium	0.30	0.14	0.14	0.14
High	0.13	0.38	0.19	0.20
	($p = 0.04$)	($p = 0.00$)	($p = 0.95$)	($p = 0.65$)
Predominant religion				
Muslim	0.44	0.14	0.18	0.11
Christian	0.21	0.28	0.00	0.00
Buddhist	0.09	0.05	0.44	0.44
Hindu	0.06	0.06	0.00	0.00
Mixed/other	0.31	0.32	0.61	0.65
	($p = 0.26$)	($p = 0.01$)	($p = 0.00$)	($p = 0.00$)

(continued)

Table 2.3 Continued

Country characteristic	All events		Suicide attacks	
	Origin	*Target*	*Origin*	*Target*
Mountainous terrain				
Under median	0.27	0.19	0.23	0.25
Above median	0.35	0.29	0.12	0.06
	($p = 0.41$)	($p = 0.60$)	($p = 0.61$)	($p = 0.18$)
Ethnolinguistic fractionalization				
Under median	0.22	0.21	0.30	0.26
Above median	0.31	0.23	0.00	0.01
	($p = 0.47$)	($p = 0.52$)	($p = 0.00$)	($p = 0.00$)
Religious fractionalization				
Under median	0.23	0.23	0.17	0.17
Above median	0.31	0.23	0.15	0.12
	($p = 0.52$)	($p = 0.84$)	($p = 0.96$)	($p = 0.72$)

Source: Krueger and Laitin (2007).
Notes: Sample sizes range from 135 to 159 depending on characteristic. The numbers in parentheses are the p-values for a χ^2 test of the hypothesis that the groups have equal effects from a negative binomial regression of the number of events on indicators for the specified groups and log population, constraining the coefficient on population to equal 1.

ences in the data is higher. For example, the pattern by GDP of the country of origin of the perpetrators for all events appears to be fairly uniform: we cannot reject chance as the source of the differences in terrorism rates across countries in the four GDP quartiles.

The victims of terrorist attacks, by contrast, are much more likely to come from wealthy countries than poor countries. The same pattern applies to the targets of suicide attacks, although the perpetrators of suicide attacks are also more likely to originate from wealthier countries. The next set of rows in Table 2.3

shows that the GDP growth of the country of origin is unrelated to terrorist activity, but the GDP growth of the target country is significantly related to the incidence of attacks. Origin countries also do not appear to have any statistically significant difference in literacy, while target countries do.

We classified countries according to civil liberties and political rights using measures from Freedom House. I will explain those variables a bit later, but for now it should be clear that terrorists are more likely to come from countries that suppress political and civil rights.

We also break the data down by the predominant religion in the country of origin of the perpetrators or in the target country. When we do this by origin, we do not see a statistical difference by religion. Predominantly Muslim countries are overrepresented in this sample, but one cannot reject chance as the explanation for this overrepresentation. I will return to that finding when we estimate a more sophisticated statistical model.

There has been a good deal of research suggesting that mountainous terrain makes it easier for insurgents to retreat and remain undetected, thus raising the likelihood of civil wars. However, we did not find any connection between mountainous terrain and the origins or targets of terrorism in our data.

Now to explain our statistical models. Do not be intimidated by the math. We estimate the equation

$$E(y_{ij} \mid x) = \exp(x_{ij}' \beta_1 + x_i' \beta_2 + x_j' \beta_3),$$

where y_{ij} is the number of terrorist incidents perpetrated by people from country i on people or property of country j, x represents the explanatory variables (e.g., GDP per capita, literacy rate), i is the country of origin, j is the target country, and the βs are the parameters that we seek to estimate. The specification of the explanatory variables is exponential. In words, we estimate the extent to which various home and target country characteristics are associated with the number of attacks committed by people from one country against another.

For those readers who enjoy econometrics, we estimated negative binomial count models, using data on pairs of countries (over 11,000 of them). Most of the pairs of countries have had zero incidents (such as between the United States and Canada), but there is information in those cases as well.[2]

We dropped Israel and the West Bank and Gaza Strip from our sample because of inconsistencies in the way the data had been coded over time. For attacks in Kashmir, we assigned Pakistan as the origin in most cases. We dropped events that were mainly domestic (that is, we have no cases in which the country of origin of the perpetrators is the same as the target country), but our results are similar if these events are included. We restricted the sample to countries that had at least a million people, leaving us with 149 countries, or 11,026 pairs of countries, to investigate.

The statistical estimates are summarized in Table 2.4. Appendix 2.1 contains a detailed set of the underlying estimates.

First of all, we found that the income of the target country mattered. The double plus signs in the table indicate that richer countries are more likely to be targets of terrorism. That finding still holds true if you drop the United States from this dataset, in order to control for any potential bias the U.S. State Department may have introduced in collecting the data. By contrast, we do not find any effect of the income of the origin country.

Figure 2.2 presents a more elaborate look at the data along income lines. We divided countries into income quartiles according to the distribution of GDP per capita. When we examine

2. I think this is an area where it might be worthwhile to apply more sophisticated econometric approaches, such as hurdle models. But then again, given their various weaknesses, it might not be worth pushing the existing data too far.

Table 2.4 Summary of Findings for Terrorism Determinants in
11,026 Pairs of Countries

	Origin country variables	Target country variables
1. GDP per capita	0	++
2. Greater civil liberties	− −	++
3. Lagged GDP growth (1990–96)	0	NA
4. Population	++	++
5. Volume of trade between countries	−	−
6. Geographic distance between countries	− −	− −
7. Literacy rate	0	NA
8. Religion of origin country	0	NA
9. Occupier	NA	++
10. Occupied	+	NA

Notes: ++ denotes a strong positive association; − − denotes a strong negative association; 0 denotes no association. A positive or negative association that is weak or particularly sensitive to the inclusion of other variables is indicated by a single plus or minus. The volume of trade and the distance between countries are variables that are specific to origin and target pairs. NA means not applicable or not a focus of the analysis. See Appendix 2.1 for an example of the underlying statistical model reflected in the table.

the income quartiles of the countries of terrorists' national origin, we obtain two important findings. First, within each of these quartiles attacks are skewed toward targets from wealthy countries. The rightmost bar is the tallest in each of the four cases. Second, lower-income countries are not more likely to be origins of terrorism. The bars are no higher in the bottom half of the origin countries than in the top half in terms of GDP per capita. These findings are consistent with the key point from the first lecture, in which we examined the characteristics of individuals who participate in terrorism. The perpetrators tend to be middle class or upper middle class, and we now see

Figure 2.2 Adjusted number of terrorist incidents by income quartile of origin and target. Negative binomial regression adjusted for population, civil liberties, and distance between countries, and normalized relative to lowest income quartile. From author's calculations.

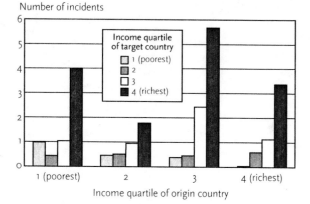

Number of incidents

Income quartile
of target country
☐ 1 (poorest)
▨ 2
☐ 3
■ 4 (richest)

Income quartile of origin country

that they are not necessarily drawn from poor countries. GDP per capita of the origin country appears to be uncorrelated with the incidence of terrorism, but terrorists do seem to target wealthier countries.

We also compared civil liberties among countries. While some of the literature stresses the importance of political rights, in actuality civil liberties and political rights tend to be highly correlated. Political rights reflect the presence of democratic practices, such as open elections, while civil liberties reflect related rights, such as freedom of association and freedom of the press. It is difficult to distinguish between the two variables, although our data suggest that civil liberties may be slightly more important than political rights. We used data from the Freedom House Index, which rates countries based on civil liberties and political rights. The civil liberties indicator measures freedom of expression, freedom of assembly, and the presence of an independent judiciary.

Origin countries tend to be countries with low levels of civil liberties. The three bars on the left of Figure 2.3 show that countries with low levels of civil liberties, such as Saudi Arabia, are more likely to be the countries of origin of the perpetrators of terrorist attacks. Countries with high levels of civil liberties are less likely to be origin countries. Within each of these groups of origin countries, countries with higher levels of civil liberties are slightly more likely to be targeted, although this is not an overwhelming effect (Krueger and Laitin, 2007).

It is also important to investigate the effect of GDP growth as opposed to the absolute level of GDP. Between 1990 and 1996, the period immediately preceding the terrorist incidents

Figure 2.3 Adjusted number of terrorist incidents by level of civil liberties of origin and target. Negative binomial regression adjusted for population, income, and distance between countries, and normalized relative to countries with lowest civil liberties. From author's calculations.

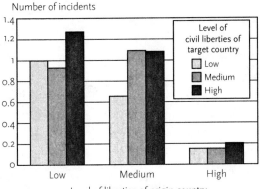

that we are studying, we find no significant impact of GDP growth on the frequency of international terrorism.

Both the population of the origin country and the population of the target country have a strong impact on the frequency of terrorist attacks. Even if India is excluded from the analysis, the pattern holds.

The volume of international trade (exports plus imports) seems to have little effect. A higher volume of trade is associated with a lower likelihood of a terrorist incident between a given pair of countries. However, the results were not always statistically significant and, most importantly, controlling for the distance between countries (because distance has a sizable impact on the volume of trade) tends to neutralize the effect of trade on terrorism. Therefore, data on the effect of trade flows might be standing in for the distance between the countries.

The effect of distance on terrorism reinforces the idea that most terrorism is local: distance seems to be a significant barrier to terrorism. Perhaps the cost of travel and the difficulty of blending into a different culture discourage terrorists from committing attacks in distant areas.

Neither the overall literacy rate nor the female literacy rate appeared to have any effect on countries' tendency to be origins of terrorism. A similar conclusion held when a country's average years of schooling was used as an explanatory variable. Consistent with the evidence at the individual level, there is little support for the belief that terrorists come from less-educated or less-literate populations.

Our results on religion pertain to the share of the people in the countries in our sample who belong to various religious faiths, not specifically to the religious affiliation of the perpetrators of terrorism. We investigated whether being home to a population with a high percentage of Muslims or a high percentage of Christians, for instance, has an effect on the likelihood of a country also being home to perpetrators of terrorism. Our results showed no significant differences across major religions.[3] Furthermore, international terrorism was less likely to occur between pairs of countries with different predominant religious groups in these data. My interpretation of these results is that religious differences are among the many potential sources of the grievances that lead to terrorism. They are not the only reason for such grievances, and such grievances are not specific to any one religion. Although the world's attention is currently focused on Islamic terrorist organizations, they are by no means the only source of terrorism. No religion has a monopoly on terrorism.

I also created a variable to identify imperial countries that occupy other countries. My hypothesis was that terrorism could be a response to occupation. I looked for data on whether country A specifically occupies country B, but I found that there are (fortunately) very few such occupations in the world today. Instead, for each country, I determined whether that country occupied all or part of *any* other country. At the same time, for each country, I determined if it was being occupied by another country. The data I obtained from this exercise were therefore not specific to the country pairings I have been using up to this point. I found that countries that occupy other countries are more likely to be targets of terrorism. Countries that are occupied are slightly more likely to be perpetrators of terrorism, but this effect is often difficult to distinguish from a chance occurrence.

Related Research

Other researchers, working with other country-level data, have generally found a pattern similar to what I have described. For example, James Piazza of the University of North Carolina, who used the same underlying State Department data as I did

3. Pape (2005) reaches a similar conclusion regarding suicide bombings.

but coded it independently and analyzed casualties as well as the incidence of terrorist attacks, also found no effect of poverty, unemployment, or economic growth (Piazza, 2006).

A recent paper by Alberto Abadie studied ratings of terrorism risk from an international risk-rating agency whose clients include international investors. He reached a similar conclusion: "terrorist risk is not significantly higher for poorer countries, once the effects of other country-specific characteristics, such as the level of political freedom, are taken into account" (Abadie, 2006, p. 51). Abadie used the Freedom House Index but focused on political freedoms rather than civil liberties, as we had done. He argued that there is a nonlinear relationship, something of an inverted U, between political freedoms and terrorism. According to Abadie, as we observe countries starting under totalitarianism and moving toward democracy, we may see a period during which terrorism increases, but after a certain point we see that more political freedoms cause terrorism to decline. However, when I plotted Abadie's relationship using his estimates, it did not seem to have an inverted U shape over the range for most countries. It mostly shows terrorism declining as steps are taken toward democracy. It is also unclear whether the proper variable to use in such analyses is political freedoms or civil liberties. The correlation between political freedoms and civil liberties is extremely high (.96 with these data), so it is very difficult to distinguish between the two variables.

The key results I have been discussing regarding terrorism are different from what one finds if one examines the occurrence of civil war (e.g., Collier and Hoeffler, 2000; Fearon and Laitin, 2003). Research that uses similar kinds of statistical models to predict the incidence of civil war in a country has usually found that lower-income countries are more likely to experience a civil war. Because of these contrasting results, it is important to distinguish between terrorism and civil war.

Figure 2.4 Countries of origin of foreign nationals captured in Iraq, April–October 2005. Released by Lynch (2005).

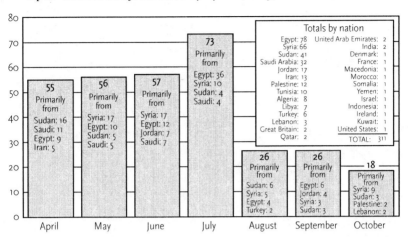

Foreign Insurgents in Iraq

I have recently conducted research on the nationalities of foreign insurgents in Iraq. The data on which I based my analysis were provided in a press briefing by Major General Rick Lynch (2005), who presented Figure 2.4, showing the number of insurgents captured in Iraq from April 2005 to October 2005. The total number was 311. (For the entire year, the total was 376, but totals by national origin were only available for April through October.) The largest number of captured foreigners came from Egypt, followed by Syria, Sudan, and Saudi Arabia. Interestingly, two of the alleged insurgents were from Great Britain, and one was from the United States.

These are the best unclassified data currently available. The original source for them, as best I can tell, was intelligence reports from the Multi-National Force–Iraq and the Multi-National Corps–Iraq. According to Major General Lynch, the insurgents are identified by their responses to interrogations, as well as by documents they may have in their possession at the time of capture. Lynch added that he could authoritatively state that the insurgents came from the countries with which they were identified (Lynch, 2005), although there is no way of independently verifying the data.

A total of twenty-seven countries are listed as countries of origin for foreign nationals captured in Iraq during this period. But there is also useful information in the set of countries from which no one was captured—presumably people from these countries were less likely to join the insurgency. To make sense of these data, I have been studying where foreign nationals captured in Iraq come from within a sample of countries in the Middle East, North Africa, Europe, and parts of Asia (including countries from which no one was captured). In some of my analyses I also limited the sample to the forty-seven countries that are within 3,000 kilometers of Baghdad. Strictly speaking the results pertain only to captured insurgents. If the captured insurgents originate from a set of countries that is representative of the countries of origin for all those who joined the insurgency, whether captured, killed, or at large, then the results can be applied to foreign insurgents more generally.[4]

Iraq is important as an object of study for several reasons. It has become a magnet for those who are angry at the United States. In addition, the invasion of Iraq has created a supply of people who are upset with the coalition forces. The U.S. government considers these data important because many officials think that a significant portion of the insurgency is composed of non-Iraqis. Although I think it is common for a military campaign to try to de-legitimize the opposition by claiming

4. This assumption may not be reasonable for all countries. For example, Egyptian migrant workers in Iraq who may have nothing to do with the insurgency may have been captured. In addition, captured foreigners may have held Syrian papers because Syria was their point of entry into Iraq, not their country of origin.

that it is made up solely or largely of foreigners, it is clear from the modest number of foreigners in the sample that the insurgents in Iraq are in fact mostly Iraqis.[5] The U.S. State Department (2006) has reported that at least 90 percent of the insurgents are native Iraqis, but many government and military officials contend that those who are carrying out the most heinous attacks are foreigners. Indeed General Lynch said, "We believe that a major piece—not numerically but in terms of the effects of their attacks—of the insurgency is terrorists and foreign fighters. We believe that they're coming—a majority of them come from Syria through the Euphrates River Valley into Iraq. Since April of this year, we have captured 311" (Lynch, 2005).

I have employed the same kind of statistical analysis that I used to study international terrorism incidents, namely negative binomial regressions, to examine the characteristics of the home countries of the foreign nationals captured in Iraq. Appendix 2.2 describes this research in greater detail. The pattern, which is summarized in Table 2.5, looks strikingly similar to that of the international terrorism incidents. I found that larger countries are more likely to be countries of origin for the foreign nationals who were captured. Distance to Baghdad has a significant effect in these models, in that countries closer to Iraq are greatly overrepresented among the captured foreign nationals. GDP per capita actually has a positive effect, implying that wealthier countries are more likely to be countries of origin for the foreign insurgents. These results contradict the view that people who are joining the insurgency are coming from lower-income countries.

---

5. This conclusion was later echoed in a declassified portion of a January 2007 National Intelligence Estimate, which stated, "*Iraq's neighbors influence, and are influenced by, events within Iraq, but the involvement of these outside actors is not likely to be a major driver of violence or the prospects for stability because of the self-sustaining character of Iraq's internal sectarian dynamics*" (italics in original).

Table 2.5 Summary of the Analysis of Determinants of Country of Origin for Foreign Insurgents in Iraq

1. Population	++
2. Distance to Baghdad	– –
3. GDP per capita	0/+
4. Literacy	0
5. Gini coefficient	0
6. Infant mortality	– –
7. Greater civil liberties	– –
8. Political rights	– –
9. Coalition member	0
10. Percentage Muslim in country of origin	++
11. Economic Freedoms	0/+

Notes: ++ denotes a strong positive association; – – denotes a strong negative association; 0 denotes no association. A positive or negative association that is weak or particularly sensitive to the inclusion of other variables is indicated by a single plus or minus. See Appendix 2.2 for details of the analysis.

Literacy had no statistically significant correlation with countries as origins for foreign nationals captured in Iraq. Nor was the Gini coefficient, a measure of the degree of income inequality within a country, a significant predictor. Higher-income countries were more likely to be source countries of captured foreign nationals, but not necessarily high-income countries with greater domestic income inequality.

If a country had a higher infant mortality rate, it was less likely to be a country of origin for foreign insurgents in Iraq. This is consistent with the perverse effect of GDP per capita, as the two variables were reasonably highly correlated, and it appeared that infant mortality was the stronger predictor of the pair.

The results for civil liberties were the same as in the international terrorism results: countries with fewer civil liberties were more likely to be source countries for foreign insurgents in Iraq. If we measured political rights instead of civil liberties, we found that foreign insurgents were coming from more totalitarian regimes. However, civil liberties were a more powerful predictor in these data.

I also experimented with adding three variables measuring the extent of economic freedom in each country in 2005, namely the World Bank's estimate of the time needed to start a new business, the World Bank's ranking of ease of doing business, and the *Wall Street Journal* and Heritage Foundation's index of economic freedom.[6] The civil liberties variable remained highly significant and sizable when these variables were included in the model. The results of the economic variables themselves did not hold out much promise for economic interventions. The *Wall Street Journal*/Heritage Foundation index of economic freedom was positively related to the number of insurgents captured, implying that greater levels of economic freedom are associated with greater participation in the Iraq insurgency.[7] The World Bank ease-of-doing-business variable was insignificantly related to the number of foreign nationals captured and the time-to-start-a-business variable was negatively related, implying that greater bureaucratic delays in one's country of origin were associated with less involvement in the insurgency.

The captured insurgents were not necessarily more likely to have come from countries that were part of the multinational coalition. I did find that insurgents were more likely to come from countries with a higher percentage of Muslims.

I believe that the importance of guaranteeing civil liberties has been underemphasized as a means of prosecuting the war on terrorism and the war in Iraq. The Bush administration has emphasized the importance of building democracy, but civil liberties can be encouraged without occupying a country in order

6. The correlations between these measures and civil liberties were .35, .61, and .71, respectively.

7. This result held whether the variable was added to the model alone or together with the two World Bank variables.

to impose democracy on it. I wrote an article for the *New York Times* in 2003 in which I argued that "a lack of civil liberties seems to be a main cause of terrorism around the world. Support for civil liberties should be part of the arsenal in the war against terrorism, both at home and abroad" (Krueger, 2003a, p. C2). Tony Blair made a similar point when he said, "The more people live under democracy, with human liberty intact, the less inclined they or their states will be to indulge terrorism or to engage in it. This may be open to debate—though personally I agree with it—but it emphatically puts defeating the causes of terrorism alongside defeating the terrorist" (Blair, 2005).

I worry that the abridgment of civil liberties at home in the United States will be counterproductive. As Benjamin Franklin is credited with having written in his *Almanac*, "Those who would give up Essential Liberty to purchase a little Temporary Safety, deserve neither Liberty nor Safety." Recall that Timothy McVeigh, who bombed the Alfred P. Murrah Federal Building in Oklahoma City on April 19, 1995, feared that the government had planted a microchip in him; he claimed he was responding to the government's actions at Waco and Ruby Ridge. The government's warrantless eavesdropping on American citizens and rampant misuse of "national security letters" to obtain confidential data are unlikely to reduce such paranoia.

I also worry about the way in which the United States is attempting to build democracy in Iraq—sometimes by destroying civil liberties. A stated objective is to spread democracy to reduce terrorism, but it is not clear whether the main determinant of terrorism is democracy or civil liberties (which often go hand in hand with democracy). This desire for democracy above all else has resulted in the curtailment of civil liberties, such as the abuses in Guantánamo Bay and Abu Ghraib. Paul Bremer, when he was director of reconstruction and humanitarian assistance for the Coalition Provisional Authority in Iraq, closed down the newspaper *Al-Hawza* because of claims that it had incited violence (Gittleman, 2004). (It has since reopened.) Perhaps coincidentally, shortly after the newspaper was closed down, there were major protests and terror incidents. Additionally, the U.S. military has been paying a company called the Lincoln Group to plant stories in Iraqi newspapers, a strategy which seems counterproductive if one wants to build civil liberties (Cloud, 2006).

Conclusion

One of the main weaknesses of the United States' war on terrorism is the government's lack of attention to data in devising a strategy and evaluating its success. I was impressed that Colin Powell wanted to solve the data problems once they were brought to his attention. I also believe that the military and intelligence agencies are genuinely interested in developing quantitative measures of their success and in using these measures to improve strategy. But we are a long way from having credible data on international terrorism, especially on trends over time.

These problems notwithstanding, neither the available microlevel data nor the more aggregated data show much of a correlation between income and the origins of terrorism. Likewise, educational attainment and involvement in terrorism, at both the individual level and the country level, are either uncorrelated or positively correlated. However, just as we often say that correlation is not proof of causality, lack of correlation does not necessarily imply lack of causality. This lack of correlation does, however, suggest to me that the burden of proof ought to shift to those who want to argue that low education, poverty, and other economic conditions are important causes of terrorism.

My research shows that civil liberties are an important determinant of terrorism. It is possible that there are some indirect links between economic conditions and civil liberties. Wealthier countries are more likely to protect their residents' civil liberties and political freedoms, so extremists in these countries might be less inclined to turn to terrorism to pursue their agendas. The data tell us that terrorism should be viewed more as a violent political act than as a response to economic conditions. Education and poverty probably have little to do with terrorism. There are many reasons for improving education and reducing poverty around the world, but reducing terrorism is probably not one of them.

Appendix 2.1: Negative Binomial Regressions for Number of International Terrorist Incidents with Origin-by-Target-Level Data

Explanatory variables	(1)	(2)	(3)
Intercept	−24.711	−24.878	−26.411
	(1.919)	(2.308)	(2.637)
Distance between origin and target countries	−0.262	−0.254	−0.233
	(0.049)	(0.048)	(0.046)
Volume of trade per capita	—	—	−0.750
			(0.650)
Different predominant religion	—	—	−0.600
			(0.239)
Origin country variables			
Log population	0.418	0.395	0.614
	(0.090)	(0.101)	(0.108)
Log GDP per capita	−0.245	−0.085	−0.189
	(−0.090)	(0.099)	(0.153)
Low civil liberties (7 = low; 1 = high)	—	0.251	0.270
		(0.092)	(0.124)
Proportion Muslim	—	—	−0.028
			(0.641)
Proportion Buddhist	—	—	−1.417
			(1.011)
Proportion Hindu	—	—	−2.475
			(1.003)
Proportion other religion	—	—	−3.026
			(1.669)

(continued)

Appendix 2.1: Continued

Explanatory variables	(1)	(2)	(3)
Female illiteracy rate (percent)	—	—	-0.002 (0.010)
Occupied	—	—	0.223 (0.523)
Target country variables			
Log population	0.694 (0.059)	0.692 (0.056)	0.646 (0.056)
Log GDP per capita	0.636 (0.044)	0.502 (0.053)	0.498 (0.061)
Low civil liberties (7 = low; 1 = high)	—	-0.167 (0.064)	-0.176 (0.061)
Occupier	—	—	0.585 (0.224)
Pseudo-R^2	0.20	0.22	0.26
Sample size	22,052	21,462	17,802

Notes: The dependent variable is the number of international terrorist events in the cell, 1997–2003. The mean (standard deviation) of the dependent variable is .03 (1.7). The average female illiteracy rate is 27.6 percent. GDP per capita is the average from 1997 to 2001 and is derived from World Bank data. The distance between countries is the distance between the origin and target countries' capitals, measured in thousands of miles by the haversine formula. The average distance between capitals is 4,482 miles. "Occupied" is a dummy variable that equals 1 if the origin country is occupied by any other country in the world; "occupier" is a dummy variable that equals 1 if the target country occupies any other country in the world. The sample excludes pairs in which the origin and target countries are identical. Standard errors that allow for correlated errors within the country of origin are shown in parentheses.

Appendix 2.2: The National Origins of Foreign Fighters in Iraq

From President Bush on down to military press officers in Iraq, the U.S. government has singled out foreign fighters as a serious obstacle to establishing stability and the rule of law in Iraq. While small in number compared with domestic insurgents, foreigners have been blamed for some of the worst acts of violence in the years since the Iraq invasion.[8] For example, Major General Rick Lynch, a spokesman for the Multi-National Force–Iraq, said, "We believe that a major piece—not numerically but in terms of the effects of their attacks—of the insurgency is terrorists and foreign fighters" (Lynch, 2005). And President Bush has stated, "Some of the violence you see in Iraq is being carried out by ruthless killers who are converging on Iraq to fight the advance of peace and freedom. Our military reports that we have killed or captured hundreds of foreign fighters in Iraq who have come from Saudi Arabia and Syria, Iran, Egypt, Sudan, Yemen, Libya and others" ("President Addresses Nation," 2005). Although reports have rightly questioned whether U.S. officials have exaggerated the role of foreign fighters (e.g., Ricks, 2006), understanding the factors that lead foreigners to join terrorist and insurgent movements around the world is an important research topic.

Foreign fighters, for example, played a significant role in opposing the Soviet occupation of Afghanistan in the 1980s and in the Bosnian conflict in the 1990s. Indeed, many of the leaders and most notorious members of the jihadist movement today were drawn from these causes, including Osama bin Laden.

This appendix is the first attempt to statistically model the origins of foreign fighters in Iraq. Specifically it presents results of negative binomial regression models estimated at the country level in which the dependent variable is the number of foreign fighters originating from various countries who were captured in Iraq according to the Multi-National Force–Iraq. The main findings are that countries with large Muslim populations, close proximity to Baghdad, a low level of civil liberties

8. According to the U.S. Department of State (2006, p. 131), "Foreign fighters are believed to number about four to ten percent of the estimated 20,000 or more insurgents" in Iraq.

or political rights, and low infant mortality rates are likely to have more of their citizens join the Iraqi insurgency. A country's literacy rate, GDP per capita, and membership in the multinational coalition are unrelated to the number of foreign fighters from that country captured in Iraq. Although the model accurately predicts the number of captured insurgents for most countries, it predicts that a larger number of Saudis and a smaller number of Sudanese would have been apprehended than was reported to have been the case. Tabulations from public opinion polls in predominantly Muslim countries, presented in the first lecture, also support the view that education and income are not consistently related to support for the Iraqi insurgency at the individual level (see Figures 1.3 and 1.4).

Data

Accurate and representative data on the nationality of foreign insurgents in Iraq are difficult to come by. This appendix analyzes data on the country of origin of 311 foreign nationals captured in Iraq from April to October 2005. The data were disclosed by the U.S. military in a press briefing by Major General Lynch on October 20, 2005 (Lynch, 2005). Unfortunately, little description was provided regarding how the data were collected.[9] According to Major General Lynch, "[Insurgents are] identified in terms of questions we asked them, interrogations we do, papers that they might have on them. But with authority, we can say they came from those countries."

The data may well contain several errors and omissions. For example, since Syria is a common entry point into Iraq, insurgents from other countries may be misattributed to Syria if they

9. It is likely that the data came from Multi-National Force–Iraq and Multi-National Corps–Iraq reports.

carry Syrian documents. In addition, some Egyptian workers who came to Iraq prior to the invasion for economic reasons may have been rounded up and counted in the data, even though they were not involved in the insurgency. And it is entirely possible that foreign insurgents who were killed in action or evaded capture are from a different mix of countries than those who were captured. Despite these flaws, this dataset represents the most comprehensive unclassified information currently available on the country of origin of foreign fighters in Iraq.

The 311 captured foreigners came from 27 different countries, summarized in Figure 2.4. The largest number came from Egypt (78), Syria (66), Sudan (41), Saudi Arabia (32), Jordan (17), Iran (13), Palestine (12), and Tunisia (10). Western countries were also represented. Two insurgents came from Great Britain and one each came from Denmark, France, Ireland, and the United States. The countries that round out the list are Algeria (8), Libya (7), Turkey (6), Lebanon (3), Qatar (2), United Arab Emirates (2), India (2), Macedonia (1), Morocco (1), Somalia (1), Yemen (1), Israel (1), Indonesia (1), and Kuwait (1).

Of course, most countries in the world are not represented among the captured insurgents, and there is information in these observations as well. Defining a universe of countries for the sample is difficult. I present results for two different samples. The first sample consists of seventy-six countries in the Middle East, North Africa, Europe, and Central Asia, henceforth called the MENAECA sample.[10] The second sample consists of forty-seven countries whose capitals are located within 3,000 kilometers of Baghdad. This is about the distance from Phoenix, Arizona, to Washington, D.C.

10. Bangladesh, Bhutan, India, Nepal, Pakistan, and Sri Lanka were included from Asia, as was Indonesia. The full sample initially contained eighty-one countries but was reduced to seventy-six because of missing data on religion and civil liberties; twenty-six of these countries had captured foreign nationals represented in the dataset.

Data on several explanatory variables—including population, GDP per capita in 2004 purchasing power parity dollars, and an index of political and civil liberties—were merged into the dataset. The explanatory variables pertain to the characteristics of the origin country. Table 2A.1 summarizes the variables, sources, and means and standard deviations for the seventy-six MENAECA countries.

Analysis

Table 2A.2 presents estimates of negative binomial regression models in which the dependent variable is the number of insurgents captured from each country. The negative binomial distribution was selected over the Poisson because the data exhibit strong overdispersion. The sample consists of seventy-six countries in the MENAECA area. Table 2A.3 presents estimates for a sample of forty-seven countries whose capital city is within 3,000 kilometers of Baghdad. (The coalition member dummy was dropped from these models because the estimates would not converge when it was included.)

The results for both samples are qualitatively similar. In all the models, the origin country's population size has a strong positive effect on the number of foreign fighters captured in Iraq, while the distance between the origin country's capital and Baghdad has a strong negative effect. A unit elasticity for population cannot be rejected in any model. The effect of distance is also sizable.[11] To gauge how much proximity to Iraq matters, consider the difference between Saudi Arabia and the

11. The depressing effect of distance is not just standing in for sharing a border with Iraq or for having to cross more national borders to reach Iraq. If these variables are added to the model in column (3) of Table 2A.2, bordering Iraq has an insignificant and small effect while the number of countries between the origin country and Iraq has a positive and statistically significant effect, and distance remains significant.

Table 2A.1 Description of Variables

Variable	Mean	Standard deviation	Source
Number of captured insurgents	3.92	13.02	Multi-National Force–Iraq
Population (millions)	39.00	128.05	CIA World Factbook
Distance to Baghdad (kilometers)	2,791	1,414	U.S. Department of Agriculture
GDP per capita ($)	$12,677	$12,076	CIA World Factbook
Percent literate	85.34	19.64	CIA World Factbook
Civil liberties index (1 = high, 7 = low)	3.47	2.06	Freedom House
Political rights index (1 = high, 7 = low)	3.61	2.30	Freedom House
Coalition member (1 = yes)	.28	.45	Congressional Research Service
Percent Muslim	42.81	43.17	CIA World Factbook
Infant mortality (per 1,000 live births)	31.34	33.58	CIA World Factbook

Note: Sample size is 76 countries in the Middle East, Northern Africa, Europe, and Central Asia.

Table 2A.2 Negative Binomial Regression Models for MENAECA Countries

Explanatory variable	Model		
	(1)	*(2)*	*(3)*
Ln population	0.803	0.784	0.737
	(0.269)	(0.241)	(0.200)
Ln distance to Baghdad	−1.833	−1.285	−0.909
	(0.519)	(0.500)	(0.465)
Ln GDP per capita	−0.153	1.142	0.062
	(0.357)	(0.478)	(0.490)
Percent literate	—	−0.024	−0.046
		(0.028)	(0.026)
Civil liberties index	—	0.454	0.530
(1 = high, 7 = low)		(0.212)	(0.188)
Coalition member	—	−0.396	−0.091
(1 = yes)		(1.010)	(0.897)
Percent Muslim	—	0.023	0.020
		(0.011)	(0.009)
Infant mortality rate	—	—	−0.057
(per 1,000 live births)			(0.020)
Log likelihood	−109.05	−96.15	−91.87
Pseudo-R^2	0.09	0.20	0.23

Notes: The dependent variable is the number of captured foreign insurgents. Estimates also include a constant. Standard errors are given in parentheses. Sample size is 76. Mean (standard deviation) of dependent variable is 3.92 (13.02).

Table 2A.3 Negative Binomial Regression Models for Sample of Countries Whose Capital City Is within 3,000 Kilometers of Baghdad

Explanatory variable	Model		
	(1)	*(2)*	*(3)*
Ln population	0.962	0.799	0.772
	(0.420)	(0.381)	(0.292)
Ln distance to Baghdad	–2.021	–2.586	–1.634
	(0.819)	(1.004)	(0.833)
Ln GDP per capita	–0.105	0.451	–0.738
	(0.654)	(0.555)	(0.575)
Percent literate	—	–0.025	–0.047
		(0.039)	(0.033)
Civil liberties index	—	0.764	0.678
(1 = high, 7 = low)		(0.377)	(0.276)
Percent Muslim	—	0.027	0.031
		(0.015)	(0.013)
Infant mortality rate	—	—	–0.068
(per 1,000 live births)			(0.023)
Log likelihood	–73.90	–63.72	–59.03
Pseudo-R^2	0.08	0.20	0.26

Notes: The dependent variable is the number of captured insurgents. Estimates also include a constant. Standard errors are given in parentheses. Sample size is 47. Mean (standard deviation) of dependent variable is 5.75 (16.26).

United Arab Emirates. The difference in the distance between the two countries' capitals and Baghdad is nearly 400 kilometers, or 0.33 units when distances are measured in natural logarithms. Based on the coefficient in column (1) of Table 2A.3, this gap would be expected to lead to nearly a 2:1 ratio (1.95 =

exp(0.33 × 2.021)) in the number of captured insurgents from the respective countries, other things being equal.

The effect of the home country's GDP per capita on the number of captured insurgents is weak and inconsistent across the models. GDP per capita has a negative but insignificant effect in the parsimonious model in column (1), and it turns positive in the model in column (2). In results not shown here, growth in real GDP per capita from 1990 to 2000 was added to the model in column (1) of Table 2A.2.[12] A country's ten-year GDP growth was estimated to have a positive but insignificant effect on the number of captured insurgents from that country. In addition, for fifty-seven countries the Gini coefficient can be included in the models in Table 2A.2. The Gini coefficient has a positive and statistically significant effect in models that exclude the percentage of the population that is Muslim, but virtually a zero effect once the percentage of the population that is Muslim is included in the model. I also find that U.S. foreign aid has an insignificant and small positive effect if it is added to the model in column (3).

Infant mortality may be a better indicator of living conditions for the lower ranks of the income distribution than GDP per capita in many countries, especially oil-rich Middle Eastern states. Curiously, a higher infant mortality rate is associated with fewer foreign nationals being captured in Iraq, and this relationship is statistically significant in Tables 2A.2 and 2A.3. The implied effect of the infant mortality rate is also very large: a reduction in infant mortality corresponding to a movement from the 75th-percentile country to the 25th-percentile country is associated with more than a sixfold increase in the number of captured insurgents. Overall there is no support for the view

12. GDP growth was computed from the Penn World Tables, Version 6.1. Unfortunately the sample size was substantially reduced by including ten-year GDP growth.

that poor or deteriorating economic conditions in the origin country lead its people to join the insurgency in Iraq, although the effect of GDP per capita is not very precisely estimated.

Many of the other variables are also of interest. A lower level of civil liberties in the origin country is associated with a greater number of captured insurgents from that country, and this effect is statistically significant in all the models. The effect of civil liberties is also sizable: the model in column (3) of Table 2A.1 implies that a decrease in civil liberties from the level of the 75th- to the 25th-percentile country is associated with a sevenfold increase in the number of captured insurgents. An important caveat, however, is that, because civil liberties and political rights are so highly correlated ($r = .96$) in these data, it is impossible to distinguish between the two variables with any confidence. The model includes only civil liberties because of the strong multicolinearity, but this variable could be picking up the effect of political rights or other factors associated with political and civil freedoms.

A higher literacy rate has a negative effect on a country's number of captured insurgents, but this effect only achieves statistical significance at the 10 percent level in the model in column (3) of Table 2A.2. Countries with a higher percentage of their population belonging to the Muslim religion tend to have more people among the captured insurgents, and this effect is statistically significant at the 5 percent level or lower in all the models. An increase in the share in the population that is Muslim by 50 percentage points is associated with a 170 percent increase in the number of captured insurgents from that country, other things being equal, according to the model in column (3) of Table 2A.2; this figure rises to 370 percent in the model in column (3) of Table 2A.3.

The final variable to note in Table 2A.2 is a dummy indicating whether each country was a member of the multinational coalition in Iraq, defined to equal 1 if the country contributed troops to the Iraq war effort (for any purpose) at any time since the start of the invasion. Participation in the multinational coalition is not associated with an increased number of captured insurgents. Madrid and London may have been targets for terrorist attacks because of their nations' involvement in the Iraq invasion, but countries that participated in the multinational coalition do not appear to be more likely to have their citizens join the insurgency. In results not shown here, I also found that the number of U.S. military troops stationed in a country had a negative but statistically insignificant effect on the number of foreigners captured in Iraq. This finding is inconsistent with the view that many foreign nationals join the insurgency in response to a U.S. military presence in their home countries.

For three-quarters of the countries in the sample, the model in column (3) of Table 2A.2 predicts the number of captured insurgents by within ±1 individual. It is informative to examine the identity of the outliers. Table 2A.4 reports information on the five largest positive and negative prediction errors. Surprisingly, the model *over*predicts the number of captured insurgents from Saudi Arabia by the largest margin. The next largest negative residual is for Iran. The model predicts a large number of captured insurgents from these countries because they are geographically close to Iraq and have large Muslim populations and a low level of civil liberties. The predicted value for Saudi Arabia is larger than that for Iran because Saudi Arabia has a substantially lower infant mortality rate.[13] The large negative residual for Iran is possibly explained by its majority Shiite Muslim population; at this time, the Shiites were less

13. If the model in column (2), which omits infant mortality, is used instead of the one in column (3) to form predictions, Iran is found to have a larger (in magnitude) negative residual than Saudi Arabia. But Iran and Saudi Arabia still have the two largest negative residuals of all the countries in this model.

Table 2A.4 Actual and Predicted Number Captured: Five Largest Positive and Negative Outliers Based on Model in Column (3) of Table 2A.2

Country	Actual	Predicted	Residual
Five largest negative outliers			
Saudi Arabia	32	136.8	−104.8
Iran	13	40.4	−27.4
Kuwait	1	10.0	−9.0
Pakistan	0	8.6	−8.6
United Arab Emirates	2	10.0	−8.0
Five largest positive outliers			
Tunisia	10	4.9	5.1
Jordan	17	3.9	13.1
Egypt	78	59.9	18.1
Syria	66	43.9	22.1
Sudan	41	5.8	35.2

likely to join the insurgency. It is also possible that Iranians operating in Iraq are less likely to be captured because of the sympathies of many Shiite-dominated Iraqi police and military units.

The finding for Saudi Arabia is more difficult to explain, and it is surprising given the amount of attention paid to Saudi insurgents in Iraq by Paz (2005) and others. Kuwait, Pakistan, and the United Arab Emirates are also predicted to have more of their citizens among the captured foreign fighters in Iraq than appears to have been the case, perhaps because of their governments' close alliance to the United States. This factor may also account for the negative prediction error for Saudi Arabia.

In the other direction, the model severely *under*predicts the number of insurgents captured from Egypt, Jordan, Sudan, and Syria. The high level of participation by Jordanians is possibly explained by the fact that Abu Musab al-Zarqawi, the leader of al-Qaeda in Iraq until his death on June 7, 2006, was from Jordan and managed to recruit many of his countrymen to his cause. As mentioned previously, the figures for Egypt and Syria may be overstated, although it is also possible that more Egyptians and Syrians have enlisted in the Iraqi insurgency than are predicted by the model. The higher-than-predicted representation of Sudanese nationals may result from the fact that al-Qaeda was previously headquartered in Sudan, as well as from Sudan's long-running civil war.

Conclusion

Though descriptive, the results in this appendix suggest that foreign opposition to the multinational forces in Iraq comes mainly from citizens of nearby Muslim countries with repressive regimes. Economic circumstances in the countries of origin of foreign fighters do not seem to be a particularly important predictor variable. Fewer Iranians and Saudis have been captured in Iraq than would be predicted by the econometric model, while more Sudanese and Syrians have been captured than predicted. Although it is possible that insurgents from some countries are better at evading capture, or that national identification of captured insurgents is biased in some ways, it is also possible that omitted factors—such as the share of an origin country's Muslim population that follows Shi'a Islam or civil strife in the country—may increase the likelihood of a country's citizens joining the insurgency. It would be useful for future work to explore these possible influences.

Another interesting question is why distance has such a large effect on participation in the insurgency, conditional on the other variables in the model. Greater distance could raise the cost of joining the insurgency, although travel to Iraq is probably not prohibitively expensive. Another possibility is that geography matters because Iraq's neighbors feel greater allegiance to the cause of the Iraqi insurgents, or that they and their families will benefit from their involvement in Iraq because of their proximity to the country, if Iraq moves politically in the direction that they support.

Finally, it is worth contrasting the results of this study with related cross-country analyses of terrorism and civil war. On the one hand, Collier and Hoeffler (2000) and Fearon and Laitin (2003) find that the incidence of civil war falls with GDP per capita across countries. On the other hand, the material in this lecture and earlier work by Krueger and Malečková (2003), Abadie (2006), Piazza (2006), and Krueger and Laitin (2007) find that the occurrence of terrorism is mostly unrelated to GDP in the origin country and positively related to GDP in the target country. In addition, a low level of civil and political freedoms has been found to be positively related to terrorism. With these findings in mind, participation of foreign nationals in the Iraqi insurgency appears to more closely reflect the forces associated with involvement in international terrorism than those associated with the outbreak of civil war. This conclusion is consistent with the widespread belief that the objectives and motives of foreign insurgents in Iraq are different from those of the indigenous insurgents, who are waging a civil war by the standard academic definition of the term.

3

What Does Terrorism Accomplish? Economic, Psychological, and Political Consequences of Terrorism

THE FIRST LECTURE summarized micro-level evidence on participation in terrorism. The second examined terrorism at a more aggregate level, determining which countries tend to be origins for terrorists and which ones tend to be targets of terrorism. In this third lecture I consider the consequences of terrorism. This is the area where I personally have done the least research. I offer my interpretation of the literature, referring along the way to some of the work that I have done. I focus first on the economic consequences of terrorist attacks. Then I turn to their psychological consequences, followed by some comments about the role of the media. I also put the threat of terrorism into perspective by comparing it with other risks that we as a nation have faced and placing it in historical context. Finally I discuss the political impact of terrorism on the target country.

Economic Consequences of Terrorism: Small Effect or Big Effect?

There are two views on the impact of terrorism on modern economies like the United States. One is that the phenomenon of terrorism has a small effect on the economy—a theory espoused by Gary Becker and Kevin Murphy of the University of Chicago (Becker and Murphy, 2001), and by me for some time (Krueger, 2001). The second view is that terrorism has a big effect. Alberto Abadie of the Kennedy School at Harvard and Javier Gardeazabal of the University of the Basque Country take that position, as did I and Gary Becker (Becker, 2001; Krueger, 2001; Abadie and Gardeazabal, 2003). Both Gary Becker and I have been on both sides of the argument. Let us assess each argument in turn.

The "Small Effect" View

The theoretical argument for the "small effect" view is that terrorist attacks typically have little impact on the amount of physical or human capital that is available for production. In modern economies, human capital is primarily responsible for the high levels of GDP. Buildings can be rebuilt. Roads can be repaved. New cars and airplanes can be manufactured. The important thing is to protect people, for people possess the knowledge of how to produce all of these items. Fortunately most of the terrorist attacks we have witnessed so far have *not* resulted in large numbers of casualties compared to the population.

A second theoretical consideration is that there is a great deal of scope for substitution among factors of production. For example, after the September 11 attacks on New York City, a good deal of the physical space occupied by the finance industry was destroyed or rendered uninhabitable. In response to this setback, many of the investment banks, hedge funds, and architecture firms located in lower Manhattan moved into hotel rooms, which had been left vacant because people were afraid to travel. This example illustrates a shock to the way in which companies did business and the way in which they adapted, finding other ways of producing the same output by taking advantage of other resources. After the attacks, companies also made better use of space that they had not been using efficiently before September 11, such as basements. The opportunity and ability to substitute inputs is one way in which the effect of terrorism is mitigated. In addition, the defense and counterterrorism industries expand in response to terrorism, mitigating the effects of terrorist attacks on the economy and employment (Berrebi and Klor, 2005).

Some evidence for the "small effect" theory comes from studies of the effects of natural disasters, which can be much more devastating than terrorist attacks. Most natural disasters in the past have had transient effects. For example, Hurricane Andrew, a category 5 hurricane that hit south of Miami in 1992, had relatively minor lasting effects on the economy. Coincidentally both Gary Becker and I (Becker, 2001; Krueger, 2001) pointed to a study by George Horwich of Purdue University of the Kobe earthquake, which occurred in Japan in January 1995. It was the most destructive earthquake ever to hit a modern city. Some 100,000 buildings were destroyed, and 250,000 were damaged. About 300,000 people became homeless and 6,500 were killed. However, fifteen months later, manufacturing had returned to 90 percent of its pre-earthquake level. Eighty percent of the stores had reopened, and there was an investment boom as homes and office buildings were rebuilt (Horwich, 2000). The cleanup after Hurricane Andrew and Hurricane Hugo in the United States tells a similar story.[1]

---

1. One noteworthy omission from this paragraph is Hurricane Katrina, which devastated the Gulf region of the United States in August 2005. Although it is too soon to tell for sure, Katrina will likely have a lasting effect on the infrastructure, population, and economy of New Orleans. It may be the exception that proves the rule, however, because any lasting effects of that hurricane on the economy will probably be the result of a lack of will to rebuild or to return to the city, based on the realization that low-lying parts of New Orleans are vulnerable to future storms. I suspect

Cities have recovered from major wars as well as natural disasters. The lore is that, after the Allied bombings in Germany, German cities recovered rapidly. That was the case in London as well.

Similarly, cities that are targets of terrorist attacks tend to recover relatively quickly and effectively. A book titled *Resilient City: The Economic Impact of 9/11*, published by the Russell Sage Foundation, found remarkable resilience in New York in the wake of September 11 (Chernick, 2005). In terms of property values, unemployment, and other factors that would presumably be affected by terrorist attacks, London was also quite resilient after the July 7 attacks, according to a statement released a month afterward by Mervyn King, governor of the Bank of England ("Britain: Economy Unfazed by Attacks," 2005).

The "Big Effect" View

The "big effect" school rests on three arguments. First, although individual companies may adapt after terrorist attacks, certain industries as a whole can be significantly affected. The travel and convention industries were devastated after September 11. On the other hand, the financial markets, which had also been targeted by the attacks, were quite resilient. If the financial sector had been waylaid by the attacks, there would likely have been adverse consequences for other parts of the economy that depend heavily on financing, such as real estate and auto sales. If certain key segments of the economy are devastated by terrorist attacks, there can be detrimental effects in related segments.

---

that the rest of the Gulf region affected by Katrina will more or less be restored to pre-hurricane status, and that its economy will approximate pre-hurricane levels.

A second line of reasoning in favor of the "big effect" view is that people may overreact in the wake of a terrorist attack, and the overreaction may be rational or irrational. Gary Becker and Yona Rubinstein argue that widespread fear of falling victim to a terrorist attack may be rational, even if people recognize that the actual probability of the event directly affecting them is exceedingly small (Becker and Rubinstein, 2004). I think this idea is a bit of a stretch. It may be easier to explain such phenomena by pointing to the limits of rationality. I do think that people might overreact to the threat of terrorism and reduce their consumption out of fear that the future will be worse than the present. A real fear in the United States after September 11 was that consumption might fall; the consumer confidence numbers were very closely watched for signs of an impending drop. Yet, contrary to the expectations of some, consumption did not in fact drop off.

Another type of overreaction through which terrorism could cause a big effect is missteps by the government. For example, one of the bigger risks for the economy about which I have written (Krueger, 2001) is that the government could crack down on immigration. For economies like those of the United States and the United Kingdom, immigration—the energy and ingenuity of immigrants—is an important source of economic growth. For the United States, immigration is a key source of highly skilled labor. Yet it has become harder for foreign students to attend universities in the United States because of the additional red tape involved in obtaining visas to attend institutions of higher learning. There are other possible governmental overreactions to terrorism, such as invading under false pretenses a country that is perceived by some to pose a threat—an action that may turn out to be counterproductive and costly.

The third "big effect" argument is based on the idea that uncertainty increases after attacks like those of September 11. Nicholas Bloom, now of Stanford University, produced data on monthly stock market volatility around key events in history. This graph (Figure 3.1) plots daily stock price movements for each month for the S&P 100, a group of large publicly traded companies. The month after September 11, which is circled in the figure, was a period of exceptionally high volatility in the stock market. This period experienced higher volatility than even the month when Enron imploded, and there was concern that corruption might be rife throughout the U.S. economy (Bloom, 2006).

What are the implications of this uncertainty? As Bloom has pointed out, companies might respond to uncertainty by pausing when it comes to investment and hiring. This could cause an economic slowdown. Of course, Bloom's work could put him in either the "big effect" or the "small effect" camp, because in his estimation the downturn, although it could be quite substantial, would be transitory. According to Bloom, a half-year's GDP growth could be erased by the uncertainty emanating from a terrorist attack.

So what is the evidence for the "big effect" side of the argument? Some research suggests that earthquakes, although they have little short-run impact on economic activity, may have a greater long-run impact. Hines and Jaramillo (2004) have found that, in the short run, earthquakes do seem to be associated with investment booms. However, in the long run, the capital stock is lower than it otherwise would have been. Investment increases to replace the capital that was lost, but this depletes savings, reducing the steady-state capital stock. Hines and Jaramillo estimate that, over the long run, earthquakes can cause about a 2 percent drop in GDP. Relatedly, Alberto Abadie and Javier Gardeazabal (2005) have argued that foreign direct investment is reduced if a country is particularly prone to terrorist attacks.

In an earlier study, Alberto Abadie and Javier Gardeazabal (2003) have put forth probably the most persuasive evidence

Figure 3.1 Monthly U.S. stock market volatility, 1962–2004. From Bloom (2006).

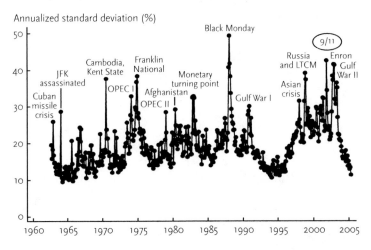

Annualized standard deviation (%)

for the "big effect" side in their studies on the Basque region of Spain. The Basque region has been the site of terrorist attacks by Euskadi Ta Askatasuna (ETA), a paramilitary group demanding independence for the region. The Basque separatist movement did not turn violent until the late 1960s, and it did not turn violent on a large scale until the mid-1970s.

Abadie and Gardeazabal studied various regions of Spain to find those that matched up well economically and demographically with the Basque region, and then used a sophisticated econometric procedure to weight the different regions to come up with a synthetic comparison region. This region was constructed to represent the path that the economy in the Basque region would have taken had it not experienced a rise in ETA terrorism. Figure 3.2 is taken from Abadie and Gardeazabal's 2003 study. The solid line in the figure shows GDP per capita for the Basque region each year in thousands of 1986 U.S. dollars. GDP per capita rose from $4,000 in 1955 to about $10,000 in 1995. The dashed line represents GDP per capita in the composite of the comparison regions. The comparison regions track the

Figure 3.2 Per capita GDP for the Basque region of Spain, 1955–1997. A 10 percent GDP gap is evident by the late 1970s. From Abadie and Gardeazabal (2003).

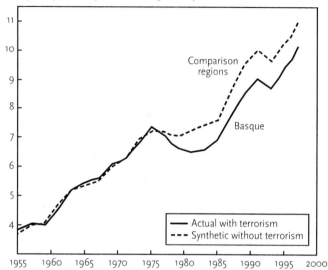

Real per capita GDP (thousands of 1986 US$)

Basque region very well in the period before the outbreak of terrorism on a wide scale, that is, until the mid-1970s. After the outbreak of terrorism on a wide scale, the comparison regions were growing more strongly than the Basque region, and by the late 1970s the gap reached about 10 percent of GDP.

If an area as large as the Basque region suffers a 10 percent decline in GDP, I would say that terrorism has had a big effect on the economy. I would define a 1- or 2-percentage-point change in GDP, especially one that is transient, as a small change. Defining the midrange would be open to debate.

Abadie and Gardeazabal found that the timing of changes in GDP lines up well with the number of fatalities from terrorist incidents. The dashed line in Figure 3.3 shows the GDP gap between the Basque region and the comparison regions, and the solid line is the number of fatalities stemming from terror-

Figure 3.3 GDP gap, 1955–1997, and fatalities from terrorist incidents, 1968–2000, for the Basque region of Spain. From Abadie and Gardeazabal (2003).

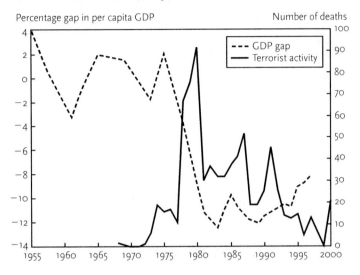

ist activity. The two measures tend to move together. We can see from this graph that the GDP gap opened up during a period when fatalities were high and rising. It would be useful to extend this type of study to other areas of the world to see how robust the findings are.[2] The trend could be unique to Spain, or it could be a significant general pattern.

Stock market event studies examine portfolios of companies or compare companies in different industries or based in different regions in order to determine the effects of various events on the stock market. Andrew Karolyi and Rodolfo Martell, two American economists, wrote a paper on the effects of terrorism on companies' stock values. Karolyi and Martell (2005)

2. Using a different approach, Eckstein and Tsiddon (2004) find that the high level of terrorism in Israel reduced GDP per capita by as much as 10 percent. See Sandler and Enders (2006) for a thorough review of the available economics literature.

used a standard stock market event model, which is based on the idea that a particular stock's movement should depend in part on how that company's stock tended to move relative to the overall market in the past, as well as current movements in the market. Their study focused on seventy-five terrorist attacks that targeted publicly traded companies. For example, a McDonald's outlet in Pakistan could be the target of a terrorist attack. They drew their data from the U.S. State Department's *Patterns of Global Terrorism Report.* For each of these seventy-five attacks they identified the company that was the target of the attack and estimated the way in which the company's stock moved compared to the overall market return in the two hundred days before the terrorist attack. They then compared the stock's predicted behavior to its actual behavior in the period just before the terrorist attack, on the day of the terrorist attack, and over subsequent days.

Table 3.1 summarizes Karolyi and Martell's findings, showing the average abnormal return for the companies in the study.[3] The term *abnormal return* refers to the difference between a stock's actual return on a given day and the return that would have been expected on that day given overall market movements. In the days leading up to the terrorist attack, the stock movements tend to be in step with the historical pattern, so there is no abnormal return. On these days the stocks experienced only statistically insignificant differences from the predicted return, as indicated by the low value of the *t*-ratios.[4] On

3. Karolyi and Martell excluded the airline companies from this sample because they thought that including them would skew the results. Airline stocks fell precipitously after September 11. Therefore, in some sense, these estimates are conservative. Airlines are included in Table 3.2.

4. The *t*-ratio is a statistic related to the likelihood that an abnormal return differs from zero by more than chance. As a rule of thumb, a *t*-ratio with a magnitude greater than 2 signals a return unlikely to have occurred by chance.

Table 3.1 Abnormal Stock Returns around the Day of a Terrorist Attack for Seventy-Five Targeted Companies

Days before or after terrorist attack	Abnormal return (%)	t-ratio
–7	–0.07	–0.1
–6	0.00	0.0
–5	0.25	1.2
–4	0.21	1.0
–3	0.21	1.0
–2	–0.39	–1.7
–1	0.33	1.6
0	**–0.83**	**–4.0**
1	0.11	0.4
2	0.16	0.9
3	0.06	0.3
4	–1.14	–1.1
5	0.46	1.2
6	–0.28	–1.3
7	–0.30	–1.0

Source: Karolyi and Martell (2005).

the day of the terrorist attack, for these seventy-five companies, the stock price falls on average by 0.83 percent, a magnitude that cannot easily be explained by chance. In the data for the subsequent week, there is neither an indication of lower growth nor a recovery in the stock price. The price seems to drop by about eight-tenths of a percentage point and stay there (Karolyi and Martell, 2005).

These numbers imply that the value of the companies fell by about $400 million for each terrorist attack. Of course, the

Table 3.2 Largest Losses from Terrorist Attacks

Company	Cumulative loss (billions of US$)
Royal Dutch Shell	10.3
British Petroleum–Amoco	7.3
Coca-Cola	4.3
McDonald's	3.7
American Airlines	2.3

Source: Karolyi and Martell (2005).

effects are not the same for all companies.[5] Table 3.2 shows the companies that suffered the five largest cumulative losses due to one or more terrorist attacks. Royal Dutch Shell, British Petroleum–Amoco, Coca-Cola, McDonald's, and American Airlines had the biggest losses in value because of terrorism over this period, based on Karolyi and Martell's estimates.

In this study, the volume of shares traded was unaffected by the terrorist attacks. In addition, the stock prices of competing companies did not appear to be affected. So, for example, on a day when a McDonald's was attacked by terrorists, Burger King's stock market value experienced no change. The stock market reaction seems to be focused on the company that was

5. During the question-and-answer session that followed my original delivery of this lecture, Sir Howard Davies, the director of the London School of Economics and Political Science and the former chairman of the Financial Services Authority (the British equivalent of the U.S. Securities and Exchange Commission), made an interesting personal observation: "One of the great modern-day urban myths is this notion that terrorists short stock ahead of the crisis. This was the bane of my life when I was a financial regulator because it was clear to me that this was not true. However, around 9/11, there had been a significant shorting of British Airways stock by the Lufthansa pension [plan], who had too much Lufthansa stock and wanted to find some way of hedging it, and happened to do this about a week before the attacks. This created a media storm, especially because no one was supposed to know but al-Qaeda."

the specific target of the attack. This is surprising to me because attacks might convey information about which particular industry terrorists are targeting. If, for example, it is perceived that they are targeting fast-food restaurants, then this news should have some impact on Burger King's stock.

In their study, Karolyi and Martell also categorized the types of terrorist attacks. The categories included the detonation of explosive devices and attacks using automatic weapons, but the one that had the greatest effect on stock market value was the kidnapping of executives. This finding is consistent with the idea that the loss of human capital has a substantial impact on companies. It is also consistent with studies showing that when the CEO of a publicly traded company dies in office there is a large drop in the company's stock market value (Schwert, 1985).

Finally Karolyi and Martell looked at the countries in which the companies were based, including their wealth and degree of democracy. They studied whether the type of country had any effect on how the market values of these companies responded to terrorism. They found that the reactions of the stock market were greatest for companies whose home bases were in democratic and wealthier countries (Karolyi and Martell, 2005). This is consistent with evidence, which I presented in the second lecture, that terrorists are more likely to select targets— individuals, companies, and embassies—from wealthier and more democratic countries. I suspect that terrorists believe they can have a larger impact by targeting such countries because public opinion in democratic countries can influence policy, contrary to the situation in autocratic countries.

Big or Small?

I would describe the effect of terrorism on the stock value of companies as small in the aggregate. For example, suppose that each terrorist attack on a company causes a $400 million loss of value. Based on the State Department data, there are on average sixteen significant terrorist attacks a year against the United States. These attacks are not only against companies; some of them are aimed at individuals, U.S. embassies, American philanthropies based abroad, or other targets. The attacks undoubtedly cause economic damage, although it is unclear if the average damage amounts to $400 million. Nevertheless, we can derive a rough estimate of the total costs of international terrorist attacks on the United States if we multiply the $400 million cost of an attack (on a publicly traded company) by the sixteen significant attacks that occur per year. This calculation suggests a loss of about $6.4 billion a year—which is quite a small share of GDP, just 0.064 percent. I would consider this to be a relatively small effect.

One could easily argue that this calculation is preposterous, because the effects of terrorism often spread far beyond just the immediate targets. The calculation misses the spillover effects —and in the next section I do consider psychological impacts, which are broader than the effects on the immediate victims. However, even if this estimate is *wildly* off, say by a factor of 30, the difference is still less than 2 percent of GDP.

In some industries, such as tourism or travel, the direct effect of terrorism is considerable.[6] In addition, terrorist organizations are adept at targeting those industries and countries that are the most vulnerable. During World War II, the American-based economist Wassily Leontief developed input-output models as an aid for determining bombing targets in Germany. To a similar effect, terrorists seem to have a sense for those industries on which they can have the most significant impact.

---

6. A well-functioning insurance market could help spread the financial risk of terrorism. See Kunreuther and Michel-Kerjan (2004, 2006) for a summary and evaluation of terrorism risk insurance in the United States.

In the end, while it is still not clear whether terrorism has a large or a small effect, I lean toward the "small effect" side. Yet I acknowledge that the evidence from Spain is reasonably compelling.

One possible reconciliation of these competing views is to suggest that, if the terrorism is as frequent and sustained as it was in the Basque region, it can have a much larger effect. September 11 was a horrific attack that created a tremendous amount of uncertainty, as Nicholas Bloom pointed out, but it did not result in a sustained level of terrorism within the United States. Bloom calculated that the September 11 attacks caused a loss of GDP of around 1.5 percent. An expected rebound after that makes the long-run effect close to zero. Economies like the United States and the United Kingdom have an advantage in that they are very diverse. These countries do not rely on critical sectors which, if damaged, could sink a less flexible economy. Since most recent terrorist attacks on developed countries have fortunately not been followed by sustained waves of equally intense attacks, most attacks probably have little effect on the national economy in their target countries.

The Psychological Impact of Terrorism

Under the definition of terrorism that I provided in the first lecture, terrorists intend their acts to influence a wide audience, wreaking fear among a broad range of people. Fear is a psychological state. To draw an inference about the psychological effect of terrorism, we can turn to statistics on objective behaviors. For example, there is evidence that after September 11 alcohol consumption in New York increased by 25 percent and doctor visits increased as well (Fairbrother and Galea, 2005). My Princeton colleague Joshua Goldstein and Guy Stecklov of Hebrew University did a study on fatal car accidents that occurred after major terrorist attacks in Israel. They found that, in the days after a major terrorist attack, the incidence of fatal accidents rose. Curiously, the number of nonfatal accidents decreased. Their interpretation was that drivers were distracted by the recent terrorist attack. The effect seemed to dissipate after a few days (Stecklov and Goldstein, 2004). Although these objective statistics represent important evidence, it is informative to explore this question further by considering data on subjective well-being and on mental health.

There is a large literature in psychology that finds that even severe changes in people's lives tend to have only transitory effects on their self-reported sense of well-being. For instance, Roxane Cohen Silver of the University of California at Irvine carried out a study in which she found that, within a month or two of having their houses burn down, subjects' level of positive emotions exceeded their level of negative emotions (Silver, 2002). People seem to quickly return to a fairly stable set point when it comes to subjective well-being.

I was interested to see if one finds the same type of phenomenon in response to terrorism. There are some phenomena to which people do not adapt, for example chronic pain. If people are struck by an ailment that causes chronic pain, it seems to permanently lower their satisfaction with life. Being laid off, especially if one is the only person in the company laid off, also has a more permanent effect on life satisfaction. However, the literature indicates that, overall, either winning the lottery or becoming a paraplegic seems to have a surprisingly small, transient effect on life satisfaction (Brickman and Campbell, 1971).

Silver and co-authors published a study in the *Journal of the American Medical Association* on the first anniversary of the September 11 attacks that investigated adaptation to those attacks (Silver et al., 2002). In order to measure the effects of terrorist attacks, Silver and her team used Knowledge Networks' WebTV service. Knowledge Networks, based in Palo Alto, California, has set up some sixty thousand U.S. households with

WebTV. Their WebTV apparatus can be used for e-mail, web browsing, or watching television, but it requires that users complete a weekly questionnaire. Silver arranged to do a survey of the U.S. population, excluding residents of New York City, to see how reactions spread outside that city after September 11. The questionnaires used a diagnostic technique that evaluates posttraumatic stress by measuring various phenomena defining acute stress, including re-experiencing a traumatic event in a nightmare or a flashback, avoidance of things that recall the event, or what is known as arousal-anxiety. People experiencing arousal-anxiety are prone to insomnia, have difficulty concentrating, or become jumpy or anxious (Silver et al., 2002). The combination of these symptoms results in an overall measure of acute stress. When Silver et al. measured stress levels two months after the September 11 attacks, 17 percent of the U.S. population was suffering symptoms of acute or posttraumatic stress. When they followed up six months later, that number had dropped to 5.8 percent.

Figure 3.4 shows only results from the arousal-anxiety component of their study. During the interval from one to three weeks after September 11, close to 60 percent of the U.S. population experienced some symptoms of anxiety or difficulty concentrating. After two months, that number had been almost halved, at 30 percent, and at six months the effect, while still noticeable at 10 percent, had significantly decreased (Silver et al., 2002). Other research finds a similar pattern.

The study by Silver et al. took into account some other indicators of individuals' background characteristics. The researchers found that the closer people lived to New York City, the more likely they were to report symptoms of posttraumatic stress. They reached the following conclusion: "The psychological effects of a major national trauma are not limited to those who experience it directly, and the degree of response is not predicted simply by objective measures of exposure to or loss from the trauma" (Silver et al., 2002, p. 1235).

Figure 3.4 Self-reported arousal-anxiety levels after September 11, 2001; people outside New York City. From Silver et al. (2002).

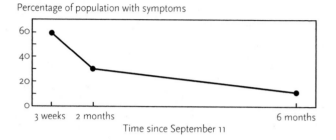

Percentage of population with symptoms

Objective measures, such as level of alcohol consumption, reinforce the conclusion that September 11 caused a good deal of psychological stress.

I have been doing some related work using a technique called experience sampling. In experience sampling, individuals carry around personal digital assistants (PDAs). Either at random or at regular intervals, the PDA beeps and asks questions like, "Just before the beep, how did you feel? Did you feel sad? Did you feel happy? Did you feel impatient to do something else?" People report the strength of their feelings on a scale, say from 0 to 6. One of the advantages of this technique is that it taps into people's ongoing experiences in real time. Data are not gathered through the filter of memory. The individual is reporting how he or she feels at that moment. Participants are not asked how they feel in general; responses to so broad a question would probably depend on how they think they *should* feel in general. Experience sampling is considered the current gold standard in the measurement of subjective well-being.

I obtained data from an experience sampling study of individuals who were participating in a smoking cessation program in Wisconsin. Unlike the study by Silver et al., this one started the week before September 11. Figure 3.5 is based on data col-

Figure 3.5 Real-time self-reported sadness levels before and after September 11, 2001; residents of Wisconsin. Data collected as part of Baker et al. (2004).

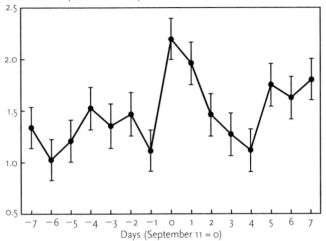

Rated sadness (± standard error)

Days (September 11 = 0)

lected by Timothy Baker and his co-authors (Baker et al., 2004). I have arrayed the data to show the week before September 11, September 11 itself (day zero), and the week after September 11. Individuals in this study were asked frequently during the day, "How sad do you feel?" The data show that on September 11 there was a large jump in reported sadness. Yet, similar to Silver's results in her work on house fires, within four days after September 11 reported sadness appears to have returned to the baseline level.[7]

In addition to asking about sadness, the experience sampling study in Wisconsin investigated levels of enthusiasm. Subjects were asked, "How enthusiastic do you feel?" The responses to this question indicate that September 11 had a greater and more lasting effect on enthusiasm than on feelings of sadness.

7. These results are not contaminated by the participants' reactions to smoking cessation; that part of the study occurred later.

Figure 3.6 Real-time self-reported enthusiasm levels before and after September 11, 2001; residents of Wisconsin. Data collected as part of Baker et al. (2004).

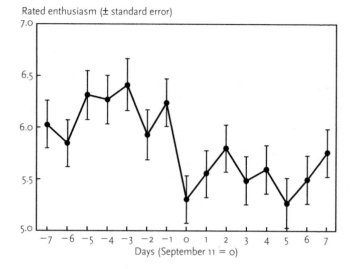

Rated enthusiasm (± standard error)

Days (September 11 = 0)

Figure 3.6 shows how people's level of enthusiasm declined, a result that is probably related to the evidence on posttraumatic stress outside New York. The drop in enthusiasm lingered at least for a time, consistent with evidence on arousal-anxiety in Silver et al.'s study.

A more common measure of people's subjective well-being is self-reported life satisfaction. Bruno Frey, Simon Luechinger, and Alois Stutzer studied data from the Eurobarometer Surveys, which ask the following question in several countries: "On the whole, are you very satisfied, fairly satisfied, not very satisfied, or not at all satisfied with the life you lead?" Responses of "very satisfied" were given a score of four; "fairly satisfied," three; "not very satisfied," two; and "not at all satisfied," one (Frey et al., 2007).

The research of Frey et al. links data from the Eurobarometer Surveys from 1973 through 1998 with information on the number of terrorist attacks occurring in various regions of France, Great Britain, Northern Ireland, and the Republic of Ireland. Because some regions within countries have historically had a much higher risk of terrorism than the countries as a whole, their analysis compared the higher-risk regions of a country to the lower-risk regions. The researchers related individuals' reported life satisfaction to their income and to the amount of terrorist activity in the region (measured by fatalities or by the number of incidents of terrorism in that year). They also controlled for overall countrywide time effects, overall region effects that did not vary with time, and certain other personal characteristics.

According to the relationships that the researchers found, a reduction in the amount of terrorism by one standard deviation, which is about eight incidents per year for England, is equivalent to moving 5 percent of the population from "not very satisfied" to "fairly satisfied" with the lives they lead. In France this change would be equivalent to moving 3 percent of those who said they were "not very satisfied" to "fairly satisfied." The figure for the Irish is 4 percent. Thus it appears that these results are similar across the three countries (Frey et al., 2007).

Do these changes in life satisfaction constitute a large or a small effect? It is noteworthy that these changes could even be measured at all, because they suggest that people did not completely return to their base levels of happiness. The authors use two approaches to scale the effects on life satisfaction that they found. First, they note that the effect of terrorism on reported life satisfaction is about a tenth as large as that associated with becoming unemployed. Unemployment is an important social problem. If the unemployment rate were 10 percent, the results of Frey et al. would imply that the threat of terrorism reduces life satisfaction by the same amount as unemployment—a significant effect indeed.

Second, the study tried to express life satisfaction differences in monetary terms. The researchers estimated how changes in income affect people's level of life satisfaction. They then computed the ratio of the estimated effects of terrorism on life satisfaction to those of income on life satisfaction. Their results imply that people in London would be willing to forego 32 percent of their income to experience the lower level of terrorism that exists in the rest of the country (Frey et al., 2007). That strikes me as an extraordinarily high and implausible number. These results may be exaggerated because the denominator of this ratio is not very clearly or persuasively estimated. Furthermore, there is a literature that suggests that people vastly overestimate the impact of income on their happiness (see Kahneman et al., 2006).

Another reason for downgrading these large estimated effects of terrorism on life satisfaction is a new study by Dmitri Romanov, Asaf Zussman, and Noam Zussman (2007). These researchers examined life satisfaction in Israel using daily data on 22,000 individuals from the Israeli Social Surveys for 2002–04. Their main conclusion is that terrorist attacks had practically no effect on the subjective well-being of Jewish Israelis, while Arab citizens of Israel reported lower life satisfaction on the days of terrorist attacks. The adverse effect of terrorism on the life satisfaction of Israeli Arabs was transitory; it was found to dissipate within a few days, consistent with the sadness results in Figure 3.5. Reported subjective well-being in Israel was stable throughout the period of the second intifada and was not lower in the most commonly targeted areas. Perhaps the results for Israel are different because the population has become accustomed to the risk of terrorism. But reported overall life satisfaction in Israel is not very different from that in the average country in the European Union, and there is no evidence of a stronger reaction in 2002 than in 2004.

Rational Fear?

As previously mentioned, Gary Becker and Yona Rubinstein have raised the question of how people respond to terrorism. They argue that people behave according to their fear of terrorism, not a calculation of the risk that they actually face. An alternate view can be based on Daniel Kahneman and Amos Tversky's prospect theory (Kahneman and Tversky, 1979). Prospect theory holds that people exaggerate the chance that an event with a small probability will occur and react more strongly to losses than to equivalent gains. Both of these factors would cause individuals to irrationally overreact to the threat of terrorism.

Becker and Rubinstein (2004) disagree with this view. They argue that people respond to the threat of terrorism rationally because fear affects people's well-being whether or not they are touched by a terrorist attack directly. In economics jargon, fear is a variable in people's utility function, and, as a result, a person's behavior is not solely governed by the calculation of the probability of an attack; instead, behavior reflects a rational attempt to alleviate the negative emotion of fear.[8]

While Becker and Rubinstein develop an ingenious model that does not dismiss the rationality of human behavior, I find the evidence for their idea to be rather weak. Instead of contradicting Kahneman and Tverksy's prospect theory, their evidence is consistent with it. Becker and Rubinstein's evidence is as follows. In Israel, after a terrorist attack such as a bombing on a bus, fewer passengers ride on buses. However, the people whose bus use declines tend to be the casual bus riders. People who use buses regularly do not take buses less frequently fol-

8. A utility function is a conceptual device for summarizing the factors that influence a person's overall well-being. Rational people are assumed to maximize their utility subject to the constraints they face.

lowing a terrorist attack. Becker and Rubinstein found the same results when a café was the target of an attack. Frequent café customers do not change their behavior.

Becker and Rubinstein's interpretation of these results is that there is a fixed cost to overcoming fear. It may be rational to have fear, but fear of terrorism can be overcome if, for example, commuters put effort into diverting their attention from the risk of terrorism. This is probably a fixed cost, as Becker and Rubinstein argue. There are, however, many different explanations for the observed changes in the composition of bus riders. For example, perhaps the people who are regular bus riders have no other way of getting to work. They do not overcome their fear in order to take the bus; they just have no other choice. Maybe they are scared but continue to ride the bus nevertheless.

I find Becker and Rubinstein's argument intriguing but not necessarily compelling. For example, one could just as easily argue that, instead of overcoming their fixed cost of fear, people who continue riding the bus or going to cafés after terrorist attacks have learned what the real risks are and have concluded that those risks are worth taking. These results could still be interpreted within the framework of Kahneman and Tversky's prospect theory. Those who continue to ride on buses might have grown to appreciate that the risk they face is small because the probability of being on a bus that is targeted by an attack is low, while those who refrain from riding on buses might be irrational, emotional responders. Those who avoid buses may do so irrationally, because they overestimate the chance of an attack, as predicted by prospect theory.

Regardless of the reason, I find it encouraging that Becker and Rubinstein's research suggests that the fear that spreads throughout the population following terrorist attacks, whether rational or irrational, can be overcome. Under prospect theory, fear would be overcome if passengers learned that the true chance of a terrorist attack is less than they first believed.

Under Becker and Rubinstein's model, fear is overcome if passengers devote effort to training their minds to be less distracted by the threat of terrorism.[9] My own suspicion is that fear of terrorism is often due to a lack of understanding of the actual risk that terrorism poses or to people's inability to put that risk into context, a topic to which I will return below.

Political Effects of Terrorism

The aim of terrorism is to further political goals, such as causing an occupying army to withdraw, influencing the outcome of an election, or replacing an autocracy with a theocracy. By sowing fear in the population, and perhaps engendering anger or frustration with a specific political party, terrorists may cause voters to elect a new government or to pressure an existing government to change its policies. This is presumably why terrorism targets democratic countries more often than autocratic ones, as we saw in the second lecture. Democracies are more responsive to public sentiment.

Does terrorism have much effect on political outcomes? Certainly one can think of some examples of spectacular successes from the terrorists' perspective. For example, the March 11, 2004, bombings in Madrid, and the poorly handled response to them by the government of President José Aznar, very likely caused the government's defeat in the general election held three days later.[10] The bombings in London on July 7, 2005, by contrast, did not have a noticeable immediate impact on British politics. But anecdotes do not make for

9. The exact mechanism for overcoming fear in the Becker and Rubinstein model is not entirely clear. They simply state (2004, p. 9), "People can handle their fears. They do so by accumulating mental capital. Investment in mental skills, like other investments in human capital, is not a *free lunch.*"

10. See Bali (2005) for a more rigorous evaluation of the effect of terrorism on the Spanish election of 2004.

strong evidence. It is not always clear what the political situation would have been in the absence of a terrorist attack, so attributing a change in government (or the lack thereof) to a specific terrorist attack is difficult at best. It is also unclear whether a particular anecdote is representative of an overall pattern, or just an unusual event.

Fortunately, a body of research has systematically studied how political outcomes are affected by terrorist incidents. Although the research is not unanimous in its findings, terrorist attacks are in fact often found to influence political outcomes. Perhaps most convincingly, the economists Claude Berrebi of the Rand Corporation and Esteban Klor of Hebrew University find that terrorist attacks within three months of an election in Israel are associated with a 1.35-percentage-point increase in support for right-block political parties—a significant margin, given the closeness of most Israeli elections (Berrebi and Klor, 2007).[11] The electoral response is larger if attacks occur closer to an election. These shifts in voting appear to occur irrespective of which party holds office. One interpretation of their findings is that a major goal of terrorist attacks in Israel is to sabotage the peace process, by increasing support for hawkish right-wing governments. Support for this view is offered by an earlier study by Berrebi and Klor (2006), which finds that terrorist attacks are more frequent when a left-wing party holds power in Israel and provides a dynamic model of the Israeli-Palestinian conflict.[12]

Recently available evidence for the United States suggests that American voters—or at least the views expressed in opin-

11. Berrebi and Klor analyze detailed geographic data on elections held in 1988, 1992, 1996, 1999, and 2003. They relate the right bloc's vote share to the number of fatalities occurring in the local area in the three months prior to the election, among other factors. Their dataset consists of 1,173 area-by-election cells.

12. A related finding by Jaeger and Paserman (2005) is that Israel regularly responds to Palestinian fatal attacks while Palestinian fatal attacks are hard to predict from the timing of Israeli violence.

ion surveys—are also responsive to the threat of terrorism. Davis and Silver (2004) found that those who perceived terrorism as a greater threat shortly after September 11, 2001, were more likely to approve of George W. Bush's performance as president. But by the middle of 2004 this relationship had reversed, and those who viewed terrorism as a more serious threat were less pleased by his performance. Eugenia Guilmartin (2004) studied the relationship between the lethality and frequency of terrorist attacks and presidential approval ratings, using monthly data from 1949 to 2002. Other things being equal, she found that approval ratings tend to rise slightly for Republican administrations following lethal terrorist attacks. Yet research on the effects of terrorism on political outcomes in the United States is still at an early stage, and conclusions may change once additional data and more sophisticated methods of analysis are brought to bear on the question.

The analysis of the effectiveness of terrorism in altering political outcomes is further clouded because terrorist organizations may not seek immediate electoral goals. For example, a terrorist organization may wish to bait a country into a long, drawn-out conflict that saps the country's will, or to derail a peace process rather than cause the current ruling party to be voted out of office. Nevertheless, the available empirical evidence provides a number of examples of cases in which terrorism has influenced political preferences and election outcomes. Therefore the conclusion that terrorism can, under certain conditions, achieve political goals deserves serious consideration. Identifying those conditions, such as the proximity of terrorist attacks to an election, should be a priority for future research.

The Role of the Media

The media play a critical role in propagating the fear of terrorism beyond the immediate area in which an attack takes place.

Because terrorist strikes themselves affect only a small proportion of the population, media coverage is essential if terrorism is to have widespread psychological, economic, and political effects. Americans watched an enormous amount of television on the day after September 11 (Figure 3.7). Almost half of the U.S. population watched at least eight hours of television news. Eighty-three percent watched four or more hours (Schuster et al., 2001). Because terrorist attacks immediately result in increased viewer attention to the media, the content of that media is extremely important. It can be expected that the initial reporting will be inaccurate. I have several theories on why the media are inaccurate in their initial reporting, as well as a few examples.

To begin with, media outlets have a strong incentive to be the first to break a story, especially in television. Each television station wants to draw viewers away from other stations, an objective that tends to prioritize speed of delivery over quality of information. Second, television does not place high priority on the accountability of experts or anonymous sources. Experts can be dead wrong, but they are rarely called to account. Third, there is the often unavoidable need for government secrecy. In order to track down the terrorists who carried out a particular attack, the government cannot reveal all its information to the media. Indeed it sometimes engages in deliberate public deception—possibly for legitimate reasons—and this obviously affects the accuracy of media reports. This occurs, for example, when the government puts out a false story in order to avoid widespread panic. Fourth, terrorist groups also have an incentive to distort coverage of attacks. Compounding all these factors and magnifying the inaccuracy of media reports is the enormous amount of confusion that typically accompanies terrorist attacks.

Since the media are prone to so many sources of error in reporting breaking news of terrorist attacks, I recommend that

Figure 3.7 Hours of television news watched on September 12, 2001. From Schuster et al. (2001).

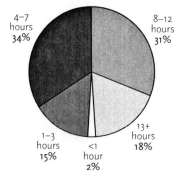

the public discount early reporting on them as a general rule. Of course, people should still pay attention to the news in case they are at risk, especially for biological and chemical terrorism. But not all news reports should be taken literally. I believe the government also has an important role here: it should try to better educate the public and media about coping with and recognizing terrorist attacks *in general,* while neither confirming nor denying information or reporting casualty statistics for *specific* incidents unless it can do so with a high degree of certainty.

Examples of Misreporting

The media have made mistakes in reporting virtually all of the major recent terrorist attacks. Here I summarize some of those mistakes to illustrate some general lessons.

The Associated Press ran a story on July 7, 2005, according to which "Police said there had been no warning that the blasts at three subway stations went off within 26 minutes starting at 8:51 a.m. in an underground train just outside the financial district. Authorities initially blamed a power surge but realized it was a terror attack after the bus bombing near the British Museum at 9:47 a.m." We now know that the bombings occurred within fifty seconds of each other. In addition, there remains some question as to whether the authorities initially believed there was a power surge or whether that was a false story intentionally spread to help maintain calm. Furthermore, it was initially claimed that the authorities had no information on the known perpetrators of the attacks. The authorities said that the attackers had "clean skins," but it was later disclosed that at least two members of the group had already been under surveillance.

It is not unusual for reporters to be wrong about the strength or sophistication of terrorist attacks. It is also common for them to be wrong about the origin of the perpetrators and the target of the attack.

In reporting the March 11, 2004, attacks in Madrid, for example, news reports around the world called the attacks the "deadliest attack ever by the Basque separatist group ETA" ("Madrid Hit by Terrorist Rail Bombs," 2004). We now know, of course, that the attacks were not perpetrated by ETA.

On September 11, CNN initially reported that there was an explosion on Capitol Hill. ABC News reported that a car bomb exploded outside the State Department. Neither of these events actually happened. When Timothy McVeigh bombed the Alfred P. Murrah Federal Building in Oklahoma City on April 19, 1995, the *New York Daily News* wrote that "the FBI reportedly was seeking three men of apparently Middle Eastern descent seen fleeing the bombing scene as a memo indicated that investigators were looking at the terror group Islamic Jihad" (Hester and Eisenstadt, 1995). Even though accurate information on the perpetrators of these attacks was eventually disclosed, there was initially a tremendous amount of misinformation.

Many terrorist organizations are quite media savvy. There is a regular press cycle, and to be included in the next day's newspaper, it helps to have your story out early in the day. To see if terrorist attacks might be timed to achieve an optimal impact in terms of news coverage, I used data from the National Counterterrorism Center's Worldwide Incident Tracking System, the government's main public database on international terrorist incidents, to compute the diurnal cycle of terrorist attacks.

Figure 3.8 shows my tabulation of the number of major terrorist attacks that occurred each hour of the day in 2004 and 2005. The figure indicates a bimodal distribution, with the largest number of attacks occurring in the morning hours and in the evening. Figure 3.9 shows the same tabulation for the subset of attacks that occurred in the Middle East. The distribution for the Middle East is unimodal, with the morning hours being the most common time for terrorist attacks. The attacks on September 11 happened in the morning, as did the July 7 attacks in London. There may be other reasons for the large number of attacks occurring in the morning, but I suspect that catching the media cycle is a factor. Obviously, the frequency distribution of the terrorist attacks has implications for security staffing.

Even if terrorists were not media savvy, the press would still have an incentive to sensationalize terrorist attacks to keep its audience engaged. As an example, consider CNN's coverage of an incident on the evening of February 8, 2006, which caused the Russell Senate Office Building to be evacuated. There was concern because an automatic sensor had detected a possible chemical agent. The initial test was indeed positive, but a second test was negative, and a third one was still being performed when CNN brought on an expert on biological terrorism. He pointed out that, according to phone calls to the

Figure 3.8 Number of major terrorist attacks worldwide by hour of day in 2004–05, for the subset of attacks with available information. From author's calculations based on National Counterterrorism Center data.

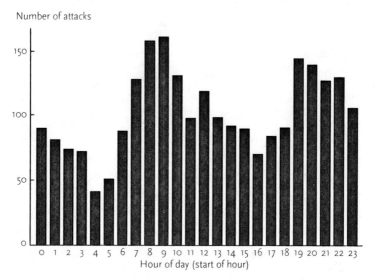

Figure 3.9 Number of major terrorist attacks in the Middle East by hour of day in 2004–05, for the subset of attacks with available information. From author's calculations based on National Counterterrorism Center data.

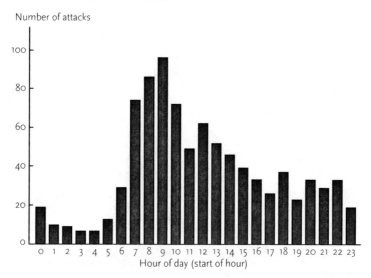

people who had been evacuated, no one was experiencing symptoms from chemical or nerve agents. He also noted that sensors such as the ones in the Russell Building frequently report false positives. A reporter, Kelli Arena, suggested that the incident could be a false alarm. Perhaps concerned that she was losing her audience, the host, Paula Zahn, then offered the following commentary:

> We just had Kelli Arena, who has reported through her Homeland Security sources for everybody to take a deep breath here and sort of hold our breath until these tests are done. . . . And yet, when you hear that you now have eight senators [the number actually turned out to be four], as well as two hundred Senate staffers who are holed up in the building parking lot, more or less—maybe quarantined is too strong of a word, but definitely holed up—it does make you wonder about this alarm, that in fact, went off in the attic of the Russell Building.

I watched for another half hour; the incident indeed turned out to be a false alarm. The evacuees were ordering pizzas in a parking garage across the street and otherwise going about their business.

Preparedness and Perspective

The U.S. Department of Health and Human Services has a guide for the media on how to understand and respond to terrorism, titled *Terrorism and Other Public Health Emergencies*. To its credit, the department commissioned this work before September 11, but it was contracted out to the American Institutes for Research (AIR), a private, nonprofit company. I learned of this because I am on the board of directors of AIR. They put together a beautiful report that is actually printed on paper that is resistant to chemical attack (United States Department of Health and Human Services, 2005). The report describes the symptoms of various types of attacks. AIR also produced a pocket guide that condenses the book and describes the symptoms to be expected from mustard gas, nerve agents, and other biological and radiological weapons that may be employed by terrorists. It provides space for local phone numbers, to be written down in advance, of emergency contacts in the event of an attack, and it provides national emergency phone numbers, such as those for the Centers for Disease Control and Prevention. This is the proper sort of preparation that can help disseminate accurate information and prevent overreaction by the media and the public.

The body of the report also contains a chart, reproduced here as Table 3.3, that puts various types of hazards into perspective.[13] It calculates the risk to the American population of dying in various ways in a given year. One in 300 people in America would die of heart disease in a year, one in 4 over a lifetime, for example. The annual risk of cancer is one in 510, pneumonia one in 4,300. The risk of anthrax (for 2001, the year that envelopes containing anthrax bacteria were mailed to the U.S. Capitol and NBC News) is one in 56 million. The probability of dying in a motor vehicle accident is one in 6,700 (United States Department of Health and Human Services, 2005). I calculated the probability of an American dying in a terrorist attack for 2005, and it is less than one in five million.[14] In 2005 the average American's chance of being killed by a terrorist was much less than his or her chance of being killed by lightning or in an airplane crash.

13. The original source of the information reported in the document is Ropeik and Gray (2002).

14. According to the U.S. Department of State (2006), fifty-six Americans were killed in terrorist attacks in 2005; according to the U.S. Census Bureau the U.S. population was 296,410,404 in that year. For the whole world, the risk of dying in a terrorist attack was one in 441,793 in 2005.

Table 3.3 Various Annual and Lifetime Risks (U.S. Population Only)

Cause of death	Annual risk	Lifetime risk
Heart disease	1 in 300	1 in 4
Cancer (all forms)	1 in 510	1 in 7
Pneumonia	1 in 4,300	1 in 57
Motor vehicle accident	1 in 6,700	1 in 88
Suicide	1 in 9,200	1 in 120
Criminal homicide	1 in 18,000	1 in 240
On-the-job accident	1 in 48,000	1 in 620
Accidental electrocution	1 in 300,000	1 in 4,000
Lightning strike	1 in 3,000,000	1 in 39,000
Commercial aircraft accident	1 in 3,100,000	1 in 40,000
Terrorism (2005)	**1 in 5,293,000**	**1 in 69,000**
Plague	1 in 19,000,000	1 in 240,000
Anthrax (2001)	1 in 56,000,000	1 in 730,000
Passenger train accident	1 in 70,000,000	1 in 920,000
Shark attack	1 in 280,000,000	1 in 3,700,000

Source: Ropeik and Gray (2002) as reported in United States Department of Health and Human Services (2005). Terrorism risk for United States is author's own calculation of fatality risk.

I think that, if the press had these numbers and really understood them, they could put the risks we face from terrorism into proper perspective. I conclude these lectures with an effort to do just that.

The Current Terror Situation Compared to World War II

To prepare for these lectures—since these are the Lionel Robbins Lectures—I went back to one of Lionel Robbins' own books, *The Economic Problem in Peace and War*, which was published in 1947 and contains the Marshall Lectures he delivered at Cambridge University that year. It is a beautifully written book. When I take an old book out of Firestone Library at Princeton, I like to look at the card in the back to see who else has checked it out.[15] I was the first person to check out Robbins' book since 1965.

In reading it, I was struck by the differences between the problems faced during World War II and those we face today. Robbins, who was John Maynard Keynes's boss during the war, writes,

> In total war, there is only one prime object of policy, the achievement of total victory. To that object, all other aims are subordinate, by that criterion, all special operations must be judged. Whatever may be the outcome of victory, whether it be a positive gain or a position perceptively worse than that from which you started, the alternative is annihilation, then, while the will to survive persists at all, no sacrifice seems too great. (Robbins, 1947, p. 47)

The risks that we face from terrorism today are not risks of annihilation. I believe a fear that exists in our society, and that has motivated some of the extreme positions taken by the Bush administration, is that terrorism might escalate to a level at which it would pose catastrophic risk. However, that is certainly not where we are today. Our current situation does not seem remotely comparable to the struggle that took place during World War II.

Terrorism, as we have experienced it so far, only matters in a big way if we let it matter. The immediate harm of terrorism is relatively small compared to the size of the economy or the population. Of course, terrorism may cause uncertainty. I do not know if the level of uncertainty is due to rational or irrational responses, but for one-time attacks it seems to me that

15. In this case, Oskar Morgenstern—co-author with John von Neumann of the theory of games in 1944—had checked out the book in 1953.

the uncertainty dissipates and does not have a lasting impact. The media need to be more responsible in reporting on terrorist attacks—to take a deep breath, as Paula Zahn herself recommended. Perhaps this could only come about if incentives were restructured so the media had more of a reason to avoid sensationalizing reporting on terrorism. Perhaps the FCC could keep track of inaccuracies in reporting on terrorism and fine media outlets if they repeatedly make mistakes. I also think that governments need to be more responsible by not exploiting these tragedies; instead they should prepare their countries to be as resilient as possible when faced with terrorist attacks.

Conclusion

When Hurricane Katrina struck the United States, we learned that multiple layers of government can fail simultaneously. The government must rehearse different scenarios in order to be able to respond adequately to natural and manmade disasters should they occur.

After September 11, New York Mayor Rudolph Giuliani's stock shot up. This is quite remarkable because just before that day he was going through a very difficult time. He was in the middle of an ugly divorce and was not popular as mayor. Yet in his reaction to the events of September 11, he projected an air of calm and was able to restore New Yorkers' faith without exaggerating the tragedy or his reaction to it. When asked how many people had been killed, for example, Giuliani replied honestly that he did not know. But, he famously added, "When we get the final number, it will be more than any of us can bear" ("It's 'More Than Any of Us Can Bear,'" 2001). That comment was soothing and reassuring to those affected by the tragedy. In contrast, faced with other terrorist attacks, for example the anthrax letters, some public officials have claimed that the situation was under control when it was not, thus losing credibility.

I recently learned that Giuliani had in fact rehearsed that line when he considered different scenarios (not limited to terrorism) that might affect New York during his time as mayor. He deserves credit for remembering it under pressure, but the important point is that his statement was not a spur-of-the-moment insight. It was the product of careful preparation—a valuable lesson.

The type of terrorism we have witnessed so far is comparable more to the situation the United States faced with the Barbary pirates in the late eighteenth century than to World War II: a risk for a small number of people that is not a major threat to most people's way of life or to national prosperity. At the same time, we certainly ought to guard against the most catastrophic threats terrorists can pose. That includes investing in radiation sensors in major population centers (although they risk producing false alarms) and paying much more attention to the enforcement of arms control agreements, to make sure that weapons of mass destruction are not available to terrorists.

It is important that policy makers not focus on the last terrorist threat but instead look forward. We must be flexible enough to respond to new types of threats. A good example of our failure to do this was the Bush administration's tragically flawed response to Hurricane Katrina. I suspect that the government's poor response, in part, was due to its allocation of excessive attention and resources to terrorism. The next threat could be domestic terrorism, a natural disaster, an asteroid, or something entirely different—we must be prepared for any of those events. Public officials in the United States must have a broader perspective, in order to prepare for *all* threats, not just terrorism.

Questions and Answers Following the Lectures

1 Who Becomes a Terrorist?

Q: Your data showing a positive correlation between education and terrorism appear to be drawn largely from Islamic countries. Evidence from these countries is contradicted by evidence from Northern Ireland, where terrorism is conducted by a maligned minority. Is it, therefore, not possible that the link between further education and terrorism is specific to Islamic countries, such as Pakistan or Turkey, and so could a solution not be more tolerant education, broader education, rather than less education?

A: You make a valid point and pose a complex question. I can tell you that the research on the Latin American terrorist organizations finds the same profile that I have emphasized. I suspect that it is very hard to change people's opinions, although I realize that education has many benefits.

The belief that more education will lead to broader consensus is a delusion. In addition, I am concerned that education in many areas does not prepare people for careers. In the second lecture I address the religious aspects of the situation, but I do not believe that any particular religion has a monopoly on support for terrorism. I highlighted Middle Eastern groups not because I think they are particularly responsible for terrorism; I did it because Middle Eastern groups are under the greatest scrutiny at the moment. I did also try to emphasize Israeli terrorists.

I view Northern Ireland as a likely exception that we do not yet fully understand rather than a case that can readily be compared to others. Even if in Northern Ireland or other countries we found a positive correlation between lack of education and terrorism, this would not necessarily imply a causal relationship. Since we did find a zero or even inverse correlation, I think it is an even bigger step to say that there could be a positive correlation in other places. On the other hand, since there does seem to be considerable support for addressing terrorism through the education system, we ought to recognize that our mission must be not only getting people into school but also examining and improving the content of the education they receive.

Q: I think Indonesia presents an interesting case worth studying. When the Asian economic miracle was going full steam, Indonesia had a kind of Islam which would be called cultural Islam, rather like the situation in Turkey. You would be hard pressed to find fundamentalism in Indonesia before, say, 1994. But when the Asian economic miracle occurred, most of the wealthy left the country, the education system collapsed, and the madrasahs that teach extremist Islam moved in from Yemen. From 1995 onward, Indonesia experienced a rise in fundamentalism. This would support your argument that it is the content of education that is so important. I think Indonesia would be an ideal research vehicle for you because it provides "before" and "after" cases.

A: I appreciate the suggestion. In the second lecture I discuss the world more generally. I could have mentioned earlier that the Palestinians are particularly well educated, but that much of their education tends to be skewed toward religious studies (e.g., Palestinian Central Bureau of Statistics, 2002). This, I think, emphasizes that it is the content of education that is relevant.

Q: I think your definition of terrorism is biased toward a Western perspective. I come from the Middle East, where there is the perception that the United States engages in terrorism by killing hundreds of thousands of people through deception and through highly advanced technology in order to achieve its goals. People who live in the Middle East, as well as those who actually become suicide bombers, strongly believe that the attacks on and occupations of countries outside their domain by the United States and its allies are the true cause of international terrorism. Why, in your definition of terrorism, is there no room at all for that side of the story?

A: I would not say there is no room for that side of the story. However, my research focuses on substate actors. As I mentioned, I do not deny that countries can engage in terrorist activity. I think that the U.S. firebombings in Tokyo during World War II, which were meant to cause fear and disruption in the society, could plausibly be called terrorism. But I think the model for state-sponsored terrorism is very different from the model for individual participation in terrorism or terrorist organizations. Because of this, I believe that state-sponsored terrorism is a different subject than substate terrorism, although I believe it too is worthy of analysis.

In addition, to a certain extent it is the victor in any conflict who gets to define terrorism. I have read that the British called George Washington a terrorist. (Under the Patriot Act, I think saying that might be a federal offense in the United States.) As I mentioned earlier, if I were to start research in this area all over again, I would avoid the word *terrorism*. In principle, I am studying politically motivated violence carried out by substate actors with the goal of spreading fear within the population and affecting more than the immediate victims. I certainly do not deny that countries can perpetrate terrorist acts and, in fact, in the second lecture I consider military occupations. If one country occupies another, or tends to occupy other countries in the world, does that make it more of a target for terrorist activity?

Q: You suggested that we might view terrorism as a particular occupational choice. If you choose to treat terrorism as a type of crime, you should study the literature that examines the effects of education on crime in general. I believe that if you look at the work that, for example, Enrico Moretti has done, there is a robust relationship showing that education actually reduces crime. Would you agree that we can see a certain tension between these two literatures?

A: The literature on crime has been able to identify education and poverty as predictors only of property crime. I think that terrorism is different from property crime. In the literature on violent crime, there is actually no relationship between economic circumstances and the likelihood of perpetrating violent crime (e.g., Piehl, 1998; Ruhm, 2000). In that sense, I think my work on terrorism is related to the empirical findings in the literature on crime. I think that literature presents a sort of puzzle. People presume that terrorism would be carried out by people who are poor and uneducated because they think of it as similar to other types of crime. I think a more appropriate analogy is voting. Terrorism is a violent and inappropriate form of political expression. I do not think this form of political expression should be tolerated, but I think that voting is a better analogy than crime. People with higher incomes and better education tend to vote more often than those in lesser circumstances because, despite the higher opportunity costs for them of voting, they perceive greater benefit from participating in the process and find it less costly to form views that they want to express.

Q: I have a question about highly educated and higher-socioeconomic-status people participating in terrorism. You said that they also tend to support more extremist positions in general. Is that true in voting, for example? Can you generalize that statement? Is it true that in Europe, where you have extreme right-wing political parties, they are supported by highly educated people, as your model would predict?

A: I am not familiar with extremist political groups in Europe, but I will tell you that, in the United States, if you look at the pattern of voting and the way people express their opinions in public opinion surveys, there exists very little connection between how people vote and their economic self-interest based on their education or their income tax bracket. If you look at extreme left-wing and extreme right-wing political groups in the United States, supporters on both sides tend disproportionately to be people who are well educated compared with the relevant population.

Q: When you talked about the role of education and the role of higher occupational levels, somebody else in the audience mentioned madrasahs and religious schools in relation to Islamic terrorists. Is there not a more aggregated variable that has a role in the occurrence of terrorism, one that might be termed "openness to information"? This might be related to education, in that the longer you stay in the education system, the more accustomed you become to taking in new information and integrating it with the way you relate to the wider world. Therefore, the longer you are exposed to that kind of environment, the more likely you are to be able to relate to and perhaps become involved in these kinds of activities.

A: I think that idea is consistent with the way I have been interpreting the evidence: that the more education people have, perhaps the more open they are to certain views, even extreme views. I think education also makes people more confident in their own views, which is one of the reasons why they are more willing to express an opinion. If you were to run a confidence scheme, like a Ponzi scheme, you would probably be more successful targeting people who are well educated and well off, who think they know what they are doing, rather than people who are less educated, and hence less self-confident and more inclined to be skeptical.

2   Where Does Terror Emerge?

Q: In 2003 you said in the *New York Times* that lack of civil liberties was a cause of terrorism (Krueger, 2003a). How do you know it is not the other way around, that terrorism does not cause a lack of civil liberties?

A: One could argue that there is simultaneous causality between civil liberties and terrorism. If a country faced some terrorist risk, it might, as the United States is doing now, curtail civil liberties. In this case, the direction of causality is backwards from what I have argued. I think that is a legitimate concern about the research findings on which I have relied. I suspect that, looking across countries in the world, most of the variability in civil liberties comes as a response not to terrorism but to other causes. However, I agree that terrorism *can* lead to a lack of civil liberties, and vice versa. This would be a useful area for further research.

Q: According to your data from 1997 to 2003, 280 terrorist events happened in India. Why do you think so many attacks occurred in this area? Could it be due to political unrest or political problems, not necessarily a lack of civil liberties?

A: I think that a large number of these attacks are perpetrated by Pakistanis. One would want to link those events to the situation in Pakistan, a country not known for strong civil liberties or strong political rights. Furthermore, both Pakistan and India are very large countries. When you scale the results according to population size, the number of attacks remains large, but it does not represent nearly as big an outlier as it might seem without taking account of population size.

Q: If you extend the dataset, which starts in 1997, it seems like terrorism runs in waves. If you were to go back a little further to, for example, the IRA's commission of terrorist acts or, even further, to the Irgun (a militant Zionist group that operated in Palestine from 1931 to 1948), do you think it would change your conclusions at all? It seems as though the time frame you have chosen is very specific to the sort of Islamist terrorism that is confined to these rebel groups. Since it seems like terrorism operates in constantly changing cycles, I believe you have chosen a very limited sample.

A: I chose this particular period because the State Department data are more comprehensive starting in 1997. The earlier reports from the 1980s were not compiled from sources that I could check for reliability. I think that extending the data would probably strengthen the conclusion about GDP per capita, especially since many of the European terrorist groups come from relatively wealthy countries. Additionally, religion does not appear to be a significant factor in terrorism in the post-1997 data. In the period that I studied, from 1997 to 2003, I do not find that predominantly Muslim countries are more likely to be countries of origin for terrorists, once I control for the other variables (Krueger and Laitin, 2007). It is not clear to me that religion or the focus on Islamic terrorism is really coloring the conclusions in the data for the period that I have.

Q: Do you have data on how many people died in these events? That information could be related to the technology used by the terrorists. If you operate at a greater distance, you try to kill many people at once. Maybe some of the trends shown in your data are due to changes in the technology of terrorism and not other determinants.

A: We do have data on the number of fatalities. I have not emphasized these numbers because they reflect a large element of randomness. For example, in the first attack on the World Trade Center ("World Trade Center Bomb Terrorizes New York," 1993), had the truck carrying the bomb been parked a little bit closer to the poured concrete foundation in the underground garage, the whole building might have come down, resulting in thousands of fatalities instead of a small number. Therefore I think that the absolute number of fatalities has a large random component. However, one could argue that more sophisticated groups are going to have greater success (and higher fatalities) even given this randomness. Piazza (2006) did look at the number of fatalities.

The idea of comparing the distance of an attack to its lethality is very interesting. I would imagine that, if terrorists are willing to bear the fixed cost of trying to mount an operation abroad, then they will indeed try to be more effective. Over time, the State Department data show that terrorist attacks are becoming more lethal (United States Department of State, 2004). It seems that the technology that is being used is now more effective. When we think about the consequences of terrorism, we need to focus on the more catastrophic events.

Perhaps that is partly what has caused the Bush administration to take the extreme measures it has. If I wanted to give them the benefit of the doubt, I would say that they have seen this trend and want to preempt terrorist activity before it gets to the really dangerous part of the curve. (Yet it is hard to give them the benefit of the doubt, given that they do not seem to have looked very closely at the State Department's data.) I think the trend is steep, but it is starting from a relatively low base. The trend is present in the data: the likelihood of fatalities from attacks has risen and the number of fatalities per attack has risen. The key, in my opinion, is to guard against *catastrophic* terrorism, not more conventional terrorism. I say more about this issue in the third lecture.

Q: Are you satisfied with the State Department's definition of terrorism and noncombatants? Do you think it is inclusive enough? Does it leave out important variables?

A: The State Department's definition does not trouble me so much as its implementation. My definition would exclude military targets, since I focus on civilians. The State Department probably had political reasons for amending its definition to include military targets. I do not think that this changes the results very much, and, using the data from the chronology (Appendix A in *Patterns of Global Terrorism*), one could omit military targets if one chose to.

I think the bigger problem is the inconsistency with which the definition is applied. Much of the data are gathered from newspaper reports and translations of newspapers from around the world. Newspaper accounts can be incomplete. On the other hand, if the idea of terrorism is to spread fear, terrorists want to get into the media. One could argue that, if a given attack did not get into the newspapers, it probably did not have a significant impact on the population. Yet I do worry about the thoroughness of the government's data collection.

Q: In the first lecture you mentioned that Hezbollah has a social wing. It is well known that many militant groups around the world have efficient social wings and are highly involved in the charitable sector in poor countries. Are you aware of any quantitative evidence on such activities? I am aware of only a few interesting case studies. Do you have any more aggregate or detailed data on such charitable activities? What kind of insights might these add to your analysis?

A: Eli Berman of the University of California, San Diego, focused on the social aspects of terrorist organizations and how some organizations develop into cults. Al-Qaeda does not operate as a social service provider. Hamas might have followed the Hezbollah social service model even more effectively than Hezbollah itself, since they managed to be elected to office. One could argue that, in certain cases, terrorist organizations compensate for the safety net or public services that the government fails to provide (Iannaccone and Berman, 2006). That is a role I could include in my model, probably with interesting results.

Q: What do you think is the importance of historical factors in determining the incidence of terrorism, and is there some way of measuring such factors? You alluded to imperialism, but are there other historical factors?

A: I am quite confident that historical factors do matter, whether based on accurate or inaccurate perceptions of history. Many of the incidents of terrorism that we see arise from disputes that have existed for hundreds of years. The influence of such historical disputes may explain the irrelevance of current economic conditions. Many terrorist groups harbor long-standing resentments due to events that occurred decades ago and that have festered and reverberated for years.

Q: What is your opinion on the arguments over political strategies, particularly in the United States, that create a climate of fear in order to generate domestic political support? Do you think such strategies contradict the suggestion of an intentional attempt to cook the books, as you mentioned, to reduce the reported number of terrorist attacks?

A: When I looked at the State Department's report and saw the trends in the glossy charts going down and the actual numbers in the appendix going up, I did wonder about why the government would alter the data in such a way. In this case the mistakes were due to incompetence. Nevertheless, political motivations could have influenced the incompetence in that, if someone in the administration had noticed the errors, and the errors had suggested *more* terrorist incidents than were actually taking place, the State Department would very likely have gone back and checked the data. All you have to do is watch CNN to see that there has been an increase in terrorism.

I also think that the public should demand more from the government. The U.S. government has appropriated a significant amount of money for the war on terrorism. We have restructured entire government departments. We have eroded civil liberties. We need better data in order to figure out whether our efforts are effective or not, whether we have the right strategy—or even if our policies are backfiring. The government appears to take a rather disinterested attitude toward statistics in this instance, which is extremely distressing to me. That is certainly not the way we do economic policy. We pay close attention to GDP growth, inflation, and unemployment. I call these non–statistically based policies "faith-based policy." The Bush administration has faith that it is pursuing the right strategies and does not see the need to monitor how the strategies are actually working. At the outset of the war on poverty, the U.S. government developed a means of measuring poverty (Fisher, 1992). The Orshansky poverty rate surely has problems, but it does tell us something about the incidence of poverty in this country, and the direction in which trends move. Little thought has gone into measuring terrorism in this way.

Q: What is your view regarding the effectiveness of terrorism? Terrorism is not necessarily effective even if it does receive a great deal of media coverage. I cannot think of any instance in which terrorism by itself has ever achieved national liberation. It has certainly played some small role in certain national liberations, but neither Northern Ireland nor Palestine, for example, has yet gained freedom. It seems that most of the time terrorism, even though it is publicized, does not really create any fear. Tube ridership has not decreased that much in London. It doesn't seem that people are running scared. Do you really think that there is a "CNN effect" with terrorism? Do you think that getting these things into the media and having people blow up coffee shops in the morning is really much more effective than other forms of terrorism? Do you have economic data or any other type of data on this?

A: There is a debate on the effectiveness of terrorism, about which I will have more to say in my third lecture. In short, my interpretation is that terrorism arises when there are few effective alternative means for an extremist group to pursue its aims. If a movement is strong enough to mount a full-fledged civil war, it will wage a full-fledged civil war. I think terrorism tends to arise in situations in which the odds are against the group that is perpetrating the terrorist acts. The tension between Israel and the Palestinians is an example. Israel dominates militarily. A full-fledged war was never a possibility.

Historically there were some cases in which terrorism did achieve the goals of an organization, or at least brought the organization closer to achieving its goals. You could probably say that about the formation of the state of Israel. In some writings in Britain at the end of the eighteenth century, George Washington was called a terrorist. I suspect that when future historians consider September 11, they will conclude that al-Qaeda was more successful than they had initially hoped. Al-Qaeda's September 11 attacks succeeded in maneuvering the United States into a position in which we invaded Iraq, we made fundamental changes at home that weakened our civil liberties, and we became more of a target for outrage around the world. It is hard for me to imagine what more Osama bin Laden could have hoped to accomplish, other than getting the United States out of the Persian Gulf.

In addition, terrorist organizations often have multiple agendas. If recruitment is among them, then receiving more publicity on CNN could help reach a wider audience and help in recruiting additional members. It is not obvious to me that terrorism is always a failure. It might be that terrorism is employed in cases in which success is very unlikely because the odds are already stacked against the terrorist group. These overwhelming odds may be a factor in the decision by extremist organizations to resort to terrorism as opposed to other tactics.

3   What Does Terrorism Accomplish?

Q: At the beginning of the lecture you discussed terrorism's effect on a nation's economy. I wonder if there is any relationship to the debt capacity and the finance capacity of the particular sector. You talked about the quick recovery in Kobe—but the Bank of Japan printed a lot of money after the earthquake. This is similar to the American government's large loans to the airline industry after September 11. In the days before the European Commission, the Bank of Spain probably could not have practiced such an expansionist policy to help the Basque economy catch up to the rest of the world. And given its current debt capacity, Japan probably cannot afford any more earthquakes like the one in Kobe. What do you think of the impact of these events in terms of a country's level of debt and its ability to use monetary policy to alleviate the effects of a natural disaster or terrorist attack?

A: I will pretend to be a monetary-economist for a moment. There is a strong consensus that monetary policy is much quicker to respond than fiscal policy and that it is probably a more appropriate instrument to use in response to economic shocks. The Federal Reserve did respond on September 11, closely monitoring what happened in the financial industry. Fortunately there were enough redundancies that, after a short shutdown, the financial system was restored.

I think the U.S. government made serious missteps in its fiscal policy after September 11. Robert Barro of Harvard University wrote an article in *Business Week* in which he looked for the silver lining of September 11 (Barro, 2001). He argued that the attacks and the resultant war on terrorism would provide impetus for federal deficit spending on military efforts as well as rebuilding New York and revamping the domestic aviation industry. In his opinion, this deficit spending would help to alleviate the creeping recession while crowding out "mistaken" programs such as those for education and prescription drug benefits. I believe that, after September 11, government fiscal responsibility seemed to break down, and the government was able to loosen the purse strings in the form of tax cuts and spending increases. As a result of September 11, the president's hand was greatly strengthened, and his agenda of running up deficits will cause more harm to the economy than did the direct effects of the attacks. It is important that public officials be more responsible, fiscally and otherwise, when responding to terrorism and to not exploit such tragedies to pursue their own agendas.

Q: I am trying to understand how you differentiate between a sustained terrorist campaign and a civil war, because this distinction makes a big difference in the perceptions of the perpetrators and the government. For instance, in the Basque region, perpetrators view themselves as fighting a civil war against the government or state agents. However, the government considers them to be terrorists. How do you differentiate between sustained terrorism and civil war?

A: One of the views I have tried to emphasize is that terrorism occurs when situations are not ripe for an all-out civil war. This requires me to define what I mean by an all-out civil war. I am relatively comfortable with the arbitrary but standard definition that a civil war is an internal conflict between at least two factions within a country that results in more than a thousand fatalities in a year. I do not think the Basque region ever reached this threshold. The situation in Israel and the West Bank and Gaza Strip has, at certain times, been close to that level of fatalities, if not above it. Much of the uncertainty after September 11 emanated from the concern that there would be additional attacks. We did not know, for example, whether there might be sleeper cells who would sustain the terrorist attacks.

Q: You have discussed the economic consequences of terrorism, especially the negative effects of terrorism on an economy. Yet there are also effects of terrorism in which somebody benefits or makes a profit from terrorism. What do you think about companies or countries profiting as a result of terrorism?

A: I have tried to emphasize the net effect on the country that is the target of the attacks, which I think is most relevant because terrorist groups are trying to influence that country at an economic level and at a psychological and political level. You are probably correct that, with sufficient substitution, some economic activity that would otherwise have taken place in the targeted country shifts to other countries. Because of this, worldwide GDP is probably affected even less than the GDP of the country that is targeted. In addition, some domestic industries, such as protective services, benefit as a result of terrorism. For this reason, I have emphasized net effects on the domestic economy.

There is a tendency, observed in New York and elsewhere, for these horrible disasters to accelerate changes that were already taking place. For instance, in New York City, the downtown area where the World Trade Center stood was already in the process of becoming more residential in character. I think it makes sense for that section of New York to become more residential, since business had been migrating uptown. After September 11, that process was accelerated.

Q: Have you studied the effects of terrorism on the oil industry? You mentioned this briefly in describing the costs suffered by British Petroleum and Royal Dutch Shell. I think that, in our current climate of terrorism, where the market price of oil is bid up, it might be significant to research the effects of these rising oil prices on the economy. Obviously there has been a lot of research done since the 1970s on shocks to the global microeconomy. What are your thoughts on the effect of rising oil prices in developed countries as well as in countries like Nigeria, where the infrastructure is more vulnerable?

A: I have been burned on this question before. I wrote an article in the *New York Times* summarizing some of the academic literature on oil prices and the economy, including Richard Hamilton's work, which suggests a tight relationship historically between oil prices and the state of the economy (Krueger, 2004). This is one of those cases in which measurement ran ahead of theory. There was a strong inverse relationship in the data but we never had a really compelling theory to explain *why* oil price shocks had such a significant impact on the economy. My aforementioned *New York Times* article predicted that the spike in oil prices might cause slower growth in the economy over the next few quarters. As it turns out, the economy seems to have shrugged off the increase in oil prices. The oil industry is extremely important, but it appears to be less central to the operation of the economy than it used to be. In the short run, consumers are not very responsive to oil prices.

Q: If you look one to two years out on happiness, what happens after a truly catastrophic event such as September 11 or Hurricane Katrina or the election of George Bush?

A: The evidence on Hurricane Katrina and other catastrophic events reveals a great deal of adaptation. People return to their set-point level of happiness before very long. The evidence that I cited on terrorism, with the exception of the study by Frey et al. (2007), is consistent with that conclusion.

The psychology literature indicates that people tend to grossly overestimate the effect of an election of various candidates. The so-called focusing illusion is a phenomenon in which, if you ask people ahead of time how bad an event will be, they predict the worst, but after it is over they report that it was not so bad. They adapted. People can avoid watching the news or not watch the State of the Union Address in order to adapt to a president they dislike. The studies that I cited did show a great deal of adaptation within a matter of days. My guess is that two years later you would see even less of an effect on people's happiness.

Q: Iraq is where the vast majority of terrorist attacks in the world today occur. There are several bombings every week, and this has a massive effect economically—probably tens of percent of GDP—and it also prevents the government from functioning. I suppose that, by your definition, this is a civil war because there are more than a thousand deaths a year, but it seems that tactics also make an important difference. If there were actual battles between two sides, in which the populations of entire towns were decimated, the number of casualties would be the same, but the deaths would not be as random as they are now. I believe that a more organized civil war would have a completely different effect than random acts of terror, in which anyone at any moment could be killed. Do you agree that the randomness of terror has a greater influence on its effectiveness than the sheer number of casualties?

A: I would put the origin of the Iraq invasion and occupation in the category of government missteps in response to terrorism. I attribute the losses in Iraq, to a large extent, to an irrational response to September 11. I think historians are going to debate whether the Bush administration wanted to invade Iraq before September 11, and if the terrorist attacks merely served as a convenient pretense. Even if that was not the case, September 11 made it easier for the government to decide to invade Iraq, since a large number of Americans believed (or were led to believe) that Iraq was somehow connected with the events of that day. This is one reason why I am still in both camps on the question of terrorism as having a big effect versus a small effect.

I agree with you that, for both the United States and Iraq, random bombings in Iraq are extremely costly. They will continue to be very costly for some time to come. I attribute a reasonable share of that cost to our misplaced response to terrorism.

It is difficult to classify the situation in Iraq because we know very little about the insurgency. In the documentary *The Fog of War: Eleven Lessons from the Life of Robert S. McNamara*, McNamara emphasized the importance of knowing your enemy—a lesson that he learned the hard way from the Vietnam War. The misperceptions within the American government about the North Vietnamese and what they were fighting for were remarkable and tragic. It seems to me that we are repeating the same mistakes in Iraq and that we have very little public understanding of who makes up the insurgency. I believe it is woven from several different strands.

I am content to call the overall situation in Iraq a civil war. Some groups operating there are terrorist organizations that are not part of the larger insurgency. Yet even within the larger effort, those fighting the civil war are using terrorist tactics. Even in a conventional war anywhere in the world, techniques such as bombing campaigns sow considerable fear in the public. Perhaps that is not terribly different from current events in Iraq.

Q: You started off your lectures by saying that terror is a tactic, a means to an end. You have concluded by telling us that the terrorists' ends have not been achieved. Could you give us a cost-benefit analysis in econometric terms of the means and the ends, from start to finish, of the tactics of terrorism and its consequences?

A: I cannot give you a fully specified econometric estimate, but I can say that I have come to believe that terrorism is often a rational act on the part of terrorist organizations. The cost-benefit calculations that they are doing are probably correct. This is not always true, as terror is sometimes completely random and counterproductive. Given the aims of terrorist organizations, I suspect they use the most efficient methods they have available. I say this because the organizations seem to be fairly rational in the way that they target industries and assign terrorists to tasks. It also seems to me that the timing of attacks is often rational, in that they cause a great deal of cost to the targets, compared to their own degree of sacrifice.

After al-Qaeda attacked the USS *Cole* with a suicide boat and destroyed the ship, former President Bill Clinton reportedly complained about how we launch million-dollar cruise missiles to knock out a few inexpensive tents in Afghanistan. It seems to me that the terror organizations' investment is often very low for what they receive in return. On the other hand, they also start from an extremely disadvantaged position in terms of getting what they want. The short answer is that the benefit-cost ratio from their perspective seems to be greater than one.

Q: What is your opinion on the effect of terrorism on foreign investment, especially in less-developed countries? Could it possibly be a barrier to growth?

A: The only study that I am aware of on foreign direct investment is the one by Alberto Abadie and Javier Gardeazabal (2005). Foreign direct investment is an inherently difficult issue to study because so many factors affect foreign investment flows. Abadie and Gardeazabal did find substantial effects of terror risk on foreign direct investment. Yet one must be cautious about interpreting these results.

As Mikael Lindahl and I reanalyzed results reported in the Robbins Lectures by Robert Barro on the effects of education on economic growth (Barro, 1997; Krueger and Lindahl, 2001), I learned that, when one works with cross-country models, the results are often very fragile. In the second lecture I reported results that relied on the same kinds of regression, using data that are probably less dependable than those typically used in cross-country research. (I do take some confidence from the fact that my data seemed to mesh well with the evidence at the individual level, however.) So, although the one study that I know of found a large effect, I believe that the question of terrorism's effect on foreign investment is still open.

AFTERWORD

The test of a statistical model is whether it can predict phenomena beyond those in the original sample. The test of a book is whether it gets good reviews and sells many copies. The test of scholarly research, I would argue, is whether it provides compelling answers to important questions; leads to additional, insightful research; and advances the public discourse in a positive direction. It is still early to evaluate *What Makes a Terrorist* on these dimensions—and certainly that task should not be left to the author—but the appearance of the paperback edition of the book provides an irresistible opportunity for the author to take stock thus far.

As a reminder, these are some of the main themes that emerge from the analysis in *What Makes a Terrorist:*

1. Public opinion surveys often find that expressed support for political violence and terrorism is higher among those with a higher level of education and higher family income.

2. Terrorists themselves are more likely to be well educated and less likely to come from impoverished backgrounds than the populations from which they are drawn.

3. Looking across countries, international terrorists are more likely to come from nations that suppress civil liberties and provide few political rights.

4. A nation's income per capita and illiteracy rate are unrelated to the number of international terrorists that originate from that country.

5. Terrorists are more likely to attack wealthy countries that afford many civil liberties and political rights than to attack poor countries with repressive, totalitarian regimes.

6. Distance matters: international terrorists and foreign insurgents tend to come from countries near those they target.

7. Terrorists using conventional methods need the media to propagate fear in order for their acts to have the effect they desire.

Out-of-Sample Prediction

The ink was barely dry on the first printing of *What Makes a Terrorist* in June 2007 when the United Kingdom was subjected to a ruthless terrorist attack that could easily have resulted in a greater death toll than the horrific attacks on the London transit system in July 2005. On Friday, June 29, 2007, a group reportedly comprised of seven men and one woman conspired to park two Mercedes 300Es packed with gasoline, gas cylinders, and nails in London's trendy West End, near Piccadilly Circus. The mobile phone detonators in the cars were called late at night, when thousands of residents and tourists were in the vicinity. Massive destruction and loss of life were avoided only because the windows of the two cars had been tightly shut, preventing the flow of oxygen required to ignite the bombs.

A day later, the two masterminds of the attack, Bilal Abdullah and Kafeel Ahmed, rammed a burning Jeep Cherokee loaded with gas cylinders into the main terminal building at

Glasgow International Airport. Ahmed set himself on fire and subsequently died from his burns. The public and press were captivated when the backgrounds of the alleged plotters were revealed: five of the eight were doctors and one was an engineer. Indeed, Mr. Ahmed was completing his Ph.D. in engineering at Anglia Ruskin University in Cambridge when he met Dr. Abdullah.[1]

This incident provides the first out-of-sample test of *What Makes a Terrorist*. An article by David Wessel in the *Wall Street Journal* interpreted the incident in the context of the book. Wessel wrote: "When Princeton economist Alan Krueger saw reports that seven of eight people arrested in the unsuccessful car bombings in Britain were doctors, he wasn't shocked. He wasn't even surprised." Although one should not draw too broad a conclusion from a single incident, the profile of terrorists continues to be one of advantage and education.

What Makes a Foreign Insurgent in Iraq: The Sinjar Records

To examine the robustness of the cross-country correlates of participation in terrorism, I examined the national origins of foreign fighters captured in Iraq (see pp. 81–89 and 91–104). The reader can tell that I felt somewhat uneasy drawing attention to foreign fighters in Iraq, since the Iraqi insurrection is overwhelmingly due to homegrown insurgents, that is, native Iraqis. A 2006 State Department report put the number of foreign insurgents in Iraq at no more than 4–10 percent of all insurgents. (Again, distance matters.) I also worry that claims by

---

1. As is common, the press did not get every detail right immediately after the attack. The perpetrators of the attack were initially described as doctors and other members of the health care profession. Some reports described Ahmed as a medical doctor, although he held a Ph.D. in engineering, which is probably the modal profession of Islamic terrorist groups.

U.S. military and political officials that foreign fighters are responsible for a much greater share of the chaos in Iraq than their numbers would suggest are exaggerated. Information captured by the multinational forces on a raid in Sinjar, Iraq, however, has led me to believe that the foreigners flowing into Iraq may well be responsible for a disproportionate share of the damage.

The Sinjar records are a personnel database of sorts, collected by al-Qaeda's Iraqi affiliates. The records contain information on the national origin and backgrounds of 606 individuals who entered Iraq from August 2006 to August 2007. The records have been coded, analyzed, and made publicly available by the Combating Terrorism Center at West Point (Felter and Fishman 2007). For 389 individuals, the records also contain an indication of the person's assignment in Iraq. These assignments were translated from Arabic by the West Point Center into combat roles or suicide bomber/martyr roles. There is considerable uncertainty in these data: it is unclear if the assignment was an actual one that was carried out or an aspiration on the part of the volunteer; it is unclear if there are missing records; it is unclear if there were other clearinghouses where foreigners were processed.

Nevertheless the Sinjar records provide an unusual window into the flow of foreign fighters into Iraq, one that can be used to produce a rough calculation of the share of suicide bombings that were plausibly carried out by foreigners in Iraq over a recent period. Using the records and data from the National Counterterrorism Center (NCTC) on the total number of suicide bombings in Iraq from August 1, 2006, to August 31, 2007, I calculate that 31–49 percent of suicide bombings in Iraq were possibly carried out by foreigners who passed through the Sinjar base.[2] This range is very high, but unnamed

2. I arrive at the figures as follows. According to the Sinjar records, 56.3 percent of the 389 foreign fighters who entered Iraq from August 2006 to

military officials have claimed that foreigners are responsible for far more of the suicide bombings. An article in the *Washington Post* reported that, "Based on the Sinjar records, U.S. military officials in Iraq said they now think that nine out of 10 suicide bombers have been foreigners" (DeYoung, 2008, p. A1). It is unclear how the Sinjar records could support such an assertion. By my calculations, for the claim to be correct, either about as many foreign suicide bombers must have passed through other intake areas as passed through Sinjar, or the Sinjar records were wildly incomplete.

Another finding of the Sinjar database helps explain a puzzle that was highlighted in *What Makes a Terrorist*. The statistical model used to estimate the nationality of foreign fighters captured in Iraq from factors like available civil liberties and gross domestic product (GDP) per capita predicted the data quite well, with most countries being off by no more than one individual. By far the largest outlier was Saudi Arabia. Saudi Arabia was predicted to be the origin of 44 percent of foreign fighters in Iraq because of its close proximity, high GDP, and low level of civil liberties, but according to military data the

---

August 2007 were assigned to be suicide bombers or martyrs. So 219 foreign fighters could be identified as potential suicide bombers. If the same percentage applies to all 606 nonduplicated records, then 341 would have been likely candidates for suicide bombing missions. Not everyone sent on a suicide bombing mission completes the task, however. Based on data from Israel for 2000–6, Claude Berrebi estimates that 62 percent of Palestinians sent on suicide bombing missions detonated bombs (personal communication). Those on failed attempts either backed out, were apprehended or killed, or had equipment failures. The NCTC records contain 395 incidents of suicide bombings in Iraq from August 2006 to August 2007, and the average incident involved around 1.1 bombers. Applying these figures to Iraq, 31 percent [= $(0.62 \times 219)/(395 \times 1.1)$] to 49 percent [= $(0.62 \times 341)/(395 \times 1.1)$] of suicide bombings were plausibly carried out by foreigners who passed through Sinjar. If NCTC data from September 1, 2006, to September 30, 2007, are used in the denominator to allow for a time lag, the proportions hardly change.

country was responsible for just 10 percent of the foreign captives. In the Sinjar records, Saudis account for 41 percent of foreign fighters entering Iraq. Thus the statistical model appears to have done a better job in predicting the participation of Saudis from fundamental factors, such as proximity and political repression, than the military's data on captured insurgents.

What Makes a Homegrown Terrorist

Since the book was published, I have been encouraged by an employee of the U.S. Homeland Security Department to study "what makes a homegrown terrorist." I must confess that this idea had not previously occurred to me. Are there enough homegrown terrorists to make the study worthwhile? Furthermore, while American counterintelligence agencies are focused heavily on potential Islamic terrorists, I have argued that they should expect the unexpected and be prepared for other types of terrorist groups and threats. Timothy McVeigh and other non-Islamic terrorist threats have quickly been forgotten.

Nevertheless, the question was intriguing, and it provided an out-of-sample test of the statistical analysis in *What Makes a Terrorist* as well as a new research direction. I was provided with an unofficial list of domestic Islamic terrorist groups— indeed, as if to prove the point that the list was unclassified, it consisted of links to each group in Wikipedia. The list included the so-called Buffalo Six as well as the groups behind the Brooklyn Bridge plot, the Columbus shopping mall plot, the Fort Dix plot, and the millennium bombing plot. There were more groups than I had expected, although an expansive definition of "homegrown" was used (e.g., including Toronto). Together with a research assistant, John Ezekiel, I tracked down the identity and demographic characteristics of the individuals involved in these plots from public sources and added some additional plots in which homegrown terrorists were involved, such as the first World Trade Center attack.[3] So far we have data on fifty-nine individuals, a small sample but one that is nonetheless informative. Although all of these individuals have been charged with terrorist activities, one could question whether some were serious plotters or instead were entrapped by overly eager law enforcement officials. This research is ongoing and preliminary. Nevertheless this dataset represents the first attempt to systematically study the backgrounds of the individuals drawn into homegrown Islamic terrorist plots in the United States.

I compared the backgrounds of the homegrown terrorists with those of a representative sample of 1,050 Muslims living in America who were surveyed by the Pew Research Center in 2007.[4] In many respects, the profile of the alleged homegrown terrorists is similar to the profiles of terrorists more generally. The homegrown terrorists were younger than the population, for example. The average number of years of education of the homegrown terrorists matched almost exactly that of the population of Muslims living in America, at close to fourteen years.

Yet averages can be deceiving. Figure A.1 compares the education distribution of the homegrown terrorists and all Muslims living in America. The homegrown terrorists are decidedly clustered in the middle of the education distribution, in the "some college" range. For those for whose occupation we could track down, the homegrown terrorists were primarily in middle-class and lower-middle-class jobs. As best we can tell, 22 percent of the homegrown terrorists were enrolled in school

3. In our definition of "homegrown" we require that those involved had been based in the United States when the plan was formed and did not come to the United States with the intention of perpetrating a terrorist attack.

4. I am grateful to Greg Smith for providing a tabulation of the Pew survey data.

Figure A.1 Education level of homegrown Islamic terrorists and Muslims living in the United States. Author's calculations from Pew Research Center survey of Muslim Americans and public sources.

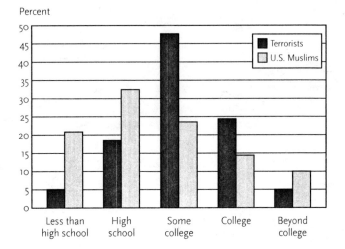

at the time of their participation, exactly matching the percentage in the population of Muslim Americans.

Other findings are that the homegrown terrorists were less likely to have converted to Islam than other Muslims in America, and this finding continued to apply if one restricted the samples to U.S.-born Muslims. The homegrown terrorists were slightly more likely to have been born in the United States than other Muslims in America (39% versus 35%), and of those born abroad the homegrown terrorists were more likely to have come from the Middle East and North Africa than other foreign-born Muslim Americans. Iran was notably underrepresented as a country of origin among the homegrown terrorists compared with the population of Muslims living in America. The homegrown terrorists were less likely to be U.S. citizens (54% versus 77%), and 22 percent of the homegrown terrorists entered the United States illegally or overstayed a visa.

How do these patterns compare with the profiles of terrorists in other countries that emerged in *What Makes a Terrorist*? Overall I interpret the profile of the alleged homegrown terrorists in the United States as tending more to the middle of the education and income distributions than that of terrorists found elsewhere. This discrepancy may result because the homegrown terrorists by and large were unsuccessful—indeed, most (fortunately) never carried out a terrorist act. Regardless of the international comparison, the hodgepodge of alleged homegrown terrorists that we studied do not appear especially deprived. These new results do not contradict the conclusion of *What Makes a Terrorist* that poverty has little to do with individuals' decisions to join terrorist groups.

Reviews

A musician-turned-author friend of mine once told me that when he reads a negative review of his work, he often finds it reassuring to read some of the scathing reviews of the Beatles that can easily be found online. Realizing that even the Beatles can be judged harshly makes it easier to cope with criticism of his own work. It has been gratifying that the initial reviews of *What Makes a Terrorist* were mostly positive; I Googled Beatles reviews only once. I was especially pleased that many reviewers praised the empirical approach to studying terrorism. David Leonhardt of the *New York Times*, for example, wrote that he considered the research "pathbreaking" and listed the book in his online column "The Year in Books, 2007."

The most interesting critique of *What Makes a Terrorist* was the suggestion that it should have been titled *What Doesn't Make a Terrorist*, for the book is more effective at ruling out explanations than it is at specifying a small number of factors that cause people across the globe to turn to terrorism. This is a fair point—and it is also revealing about terrorism itself. It is easier to take issues off the table than to identify a small set of factors that motivate ordinary citizens to become terrorists. Terrorists, by and large, are not motivated by poverty or lack of education. These "null" findings say a lot about terrorism itself and the making of terrorists. I argued (see p. 51) that terrorists are primarily "motivated by geopolitical grievances." They become fanatics willing to sacrifice innocent civilians (and sometimes themselves) because they fervently wish to pursue a grievance, either real or perceived, and because they view terrorism as their best or only means to do so.

There are myriad reasons why people have grievances. Some are nationalistic, some are territorial, some are religious, some are environmental, and so on. This is probably why poverty and the other "usual suspects" do such a poor job of predicting participation in terrorism. There is not one standard grievance any more than there is one standard profile of a terrorist. Extremists who are willing to sacrifice themselves for some cause probably exist in every large population. For this reason, I argued that the supply of terrorists is fairly elastic. Remove one perceived source of grievance and there are still others willing to pursue their particular grievances by violent means. The finite "resource" is the number of terrorist organizations capable of channeling extremists into carrying out heinous acts of terrorism.

What makes a terrorist, then, is the availability of a person with a fanatical commitment to pursuing a grievance combined with the perception that there are few alternatives available other than terrorism for pursuing that grievance, and the availability of a terrorist organization or cell willing to equip and deploy the would-be terrorist.

A second criticism of *What Makes a Terrorist* is that the screening process that selects terrorist recruits may obscure the role of poverty in increasing the supply of terrorists. In particular, if poverty drives more people to desire to become terrorists, but if terrorist organizations accept only individuals who exceed some education threshold, then the average terrorist would appear well educated, yet poverty would still tend to increase the level of participation in terrorism.[5] While this is certainly possible theoretically, and I highlight the role of both supply- and demand-side factors in participation in terrorism, I think the evidence summarized in *What Makes a Terrorist* strongly suggests that the supply of would-be terrorists does *not* increase with poverty for four reasons. First, the occurrence of hate crimes, which tend to be perpetrated by lone wolves acting on their own, also bears little or no relationship to poverty and unemployment. Second, those who are better educated and wealthier are more likely to express support for terrorist acts in several public opinion polls that have been conducted in high-terrorism regions. The selection process is not an issue when it comes to either hate crimes or responses to public opinion polls. Third, time-series analyses typically do not find that terrorist incidents rise when economic conditions turn down. Fourth, a country's GDP per capita or illiteracy rate is unrelated to the number of terrorists who come from that country, holding other factors constant. Nevertheless, the point that supply should be separated from demand is well taken and should be a focus of future research.

5. Ethan Bueno de Mesquita (2007, p. 1726) writes, "suppose that terrorist organizations accept recruits only over some competence threshold and that, as suggested by the data, competence is positively correlated with income or education. Suppose, further, that economic downturns increase mobilization (perhaps by decreasing opportunity costs). In such a world, because of screening, the terrorists actually observed will be neither poor nor poorly educated, just as in Krueger's data. Yet, Krueger's conclusion will not be true: the supply of acceptable operatives and, therefore, the expected level of violence will be affected by economic factors."

Public Discourse

The public discourse on terrorism continues to be mixed. During the 2008 presidential primaries, Republican candidates vied to be tough on terrorism while Democratic candidates addressed terrorism to a lesser extent—and the public gravitated toward the slowing economy and the war in Iraq as their major concerns.

American public officials continued to exploit terrorist fears. In a widely reported interview with the *Chicago Tribune*'s editorial board in July 2007, Homeland Security Secretary Michael Chertoff said he had a "gut feeling" that al-Qaeda could attack the United States during the summer. His logic was that "summertime seems to be appealing to them." That claim is not supported by empirical evidence, as far as I can tell. Using the NCTC data, I calculated the seasonal pattern of terrorist attacks by al-Qaeda (Figure A.2). Summertime does not leap out as a particularly frequent time for attacks. When this evidence was brought to the attention of the Department of Homeland Security, one of its spokespeople responded by attacking me.[6]

Fortunately Mr. Chertoff's "gut feeling" was wrong and the U.S. homeland was not attacked by al-Qaeda terrorists in the summer of 2007. Yet his warning—which was issued in connection with a plea to pass President George W. Bush's proposed immigration bill—was probably not without cost. Ele-

---

6. Zack Phillips (2007) of *Government Executive* magazine wrote, "DHS spokesman Russ Knocke said Krueger's comments ignore the National Intelligence Estimate released in July, 'which cites increased activity overseas as evidence of an enemy that is reconstituting. He may have also missed the news about the Glasgow plot, and the arrests in Germany and Denmark. . . . But, if any doubt lingers in his mind about activity in spring and summer months in recent years, he need only ask the families of victims from London, Madrid and 9/11.'" Evidently Mr. Knocke does not think it important to consider the victims of terrorist attacks that occurred in winter and fall.

Figure A.2 Seasonal pattern of terrorism, al-Qaeda, 2004–06. Author's calculations based on NCTC WITS dataset; 39 incidents total.

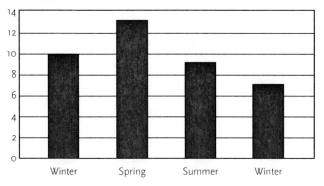

Number of incidents

vating fear for a specified period on the basis of little direct evidence could cause the government and the public to be less vigilant at other times. And fear itself has consequences. A study by Roxane Cohen Silver, E. Alison Holman, and colleagues (2002), for example, found that stress from terrorist attacks is associated with a higher likelihood of heart attacks. Stecklov and Goldstein (2004) have found that fear of terrorism is associated with higher levels of driving fatalities.

In my view, public officials should not raise the specter of terrorist acts occurring within specified time periods unless they have an empirical basis for doing so. With a change of administration in the United States due in 2009, one can hope that the public discourse on terrorism will be based more on facts and less on fear.

REFERENCES

Abadie, Alberto. 2006. "Poverty, Political Freedom, and the Roots of Terrorism." *American Economic Review* 96(2): 50–56.

Abadie, Alberto, and Javier Gardeazabal. 2003. "The Economic Costs of Conflict: A Case Study of the Basque Country." *American Economic Review* 93(1): 113–32.

———. 2005. "Terrorism and the World Economy." Preliminary draft, Harvard University.

Armitage, Richard, and Kara Bue. 2006. "Keep Pakistan on Our Side." *New York Times*, August 20, p. 11.

Baker, Timothy, Michael Fiore, and Saul Shiffman. 2004. "Pharmacotherapies: Efficacy, Mechanisms, and Algorithms." University of Wisconsin–Madison.

Bali, Valentina A. 2005. "Terror and Elections: Lessons from Spain." Unpublished manuscript, Michigan State University.

Barro, Robert. 1997. *Determinants of Economic Growth: A Cross-Country Empirical Study.* Cambridge, Mass.: MIT Press.

———. 2001. "Why the U.S. Economy Will Rise Again." *Business Week*, October 1, p. 20.

Barro, Robert, and Jong-Wha Lee. 2000. "International Data on Educational Attainment: Updates and Implications." Harvard University Center for International Development Working Paper 42. http://www.ksg.harvard.edu/CID/cidwp/042.pdf.

Becker, Gary. 2001. "Don't Be Surprised If the Recovery Is Rapid." *Business Week*, October 22, p. 26.

Becker, Gary, and Kevin Murphy. 2001. "Prosperity Will Rise Out of the Ashes." *Wall Street Journal*, October 29, p. A22.

Becker, Gary, and Yona Rubinstein. 2004. "Fear and the Response to Terrorism: An Economic Analysis." Unpublished manuscript, University of Chicago.

Benmelech, Efrain, and Claude Berrebi. 2007. "Attack Assignments in Terror Organizations and the Productivity of Suicide Bombers." Working Paper 12910. Cambridge, Mass.: National Bureau of Economic Research.

Berrebi, Claude. 2004. "The Causes and Consequences of Terrorism." Doctoral dissertation, Department of Economics, Princeton University, Proquest Dissertations and Theses Database.

Berrebi, Claude, and Esteban F. Klor. 2005. "The Impact of Terrorism across Industries: An Empirical Study." Discussion Paper 5360. London: Center for Economic Policy Research.

———. 2006. "On Terrorism and Electoral Outcomes: Theory and Evidence from the Israeli-Palestinian Conflict." *Journal of Conflict Resolution* 50(6): 899–925.

———. 2007. "The Impact of Terrorism on Voters' Preferences." Unpublished draft, RAND Corporation.

Black, Ian, and Benny Morris. 1991. *Israel's Secret Wars: The Untold History of Israeli Intelligence*. London: Hamish Hamilton.

Blair, Tony. 2001. "Speech by the Prime Minister at the Lord Mayor's Banquet." November 12. http://www.number-10.gov.uk/output/Page1661.asp.

———. 2005. "Special Address by Tony Blair, Prime Minister of the United Kingdom." World Economic Forum, Annual Meeting, Davos, Switzerland, January 27. http://www.weforum.org/site/homepublic.nsf/Content/Special+Address+by+Tony+Blair,+Prime+Minister+of+the+United+Kingdom.

Bloom, Nicholas. 2006. "The Impact of Uncertainty Shocks: Firm-Level Estimation and a 9/11 Simulation." Center for Economic Performance Discussion Paper 718. http://cep.lse.ac.uk/pubs/download/dp0718.pdf.

Boucher, Richard. 2004. "Correction to Global Patterns of Terrorism Will Be Released." Press Statement, U.S. Department of State, Washington, D.C., June 10. http://www.state.gov/r/pa/prs/ps/2004/33433.htm.

Brickman, P. D., and D. T. Campbell. 1971. "Hedonic Relativism and Planning the Good Society." In M. H. Appleby, ed., *Adaptation-Level Theory*, pp. 287–302. New York: Academic Press.

"Britain: Economy Unfazed by Attacks." 2005. Bloomberg News, reprinted in the *New York Times*, August 11, p. C4.

Bueno de Mesquita, Ethan. 2007. "Why People Turn to Bombs." *Science* 318: 1726–27.

Bush, George W. 2002. "Remarks by the President at United Nations Financing for Development Conference." Cintermex Convention Center, Monterrey, Mexico, March 22. http://www.whitehouse.gov/news/releases/2002/03/20020322-1.html.

———. 2003. "State of the Union Address." U.S. Capitol, Washington, D.C., January 28. http://www.whitehouse.gov/news/releases/2003/01/20030128-19.html.

Bush, Laura. 2002. "The First Lady of the United States Highlights the Importance of Education in Paris." Speech at the Organization for Economic Cooperation and Development, Paris, France, May 20. http://www1.oecd.org/forum2002/speeches/day2/laurabush.

Central Intelligence Agency. 2007. *CIA World Factbook*. www.cia.gov/cia/publications/factbook/index.html.

Chen, Shaouha, and Martin Ravallion. 2005. "How Have the World's Poorest Fared since the Early 1980s?" Policy Research Working Paper 3341. Washington, D.C.: World Bank.

Chernick, Howard, ed. 2005. *Resilient City: The Economic Impact of 9/11*. New York: Russell Sage Foundation.

Clarke, Richard. 2004. *Against All Enemies*. New York: Free Press.

Cloud, David S. 2006. "Quick Rise for Purveyors of Propaganda in Iraq." *New York Times*, February 15, p. A1.

Collier, Paul, and Anne Hoeffler. 2000. "Greed and Grievance in Civil War." Policy Research Working Paper 2355. Washington, D.C.: World Bank.

Davis, Darren W., and Brian D. Silver. 2004. "The Threat of Terrorism, Presidential Approval, and the 2004 Election." Unpublished manuscript, Michigan State University.

DeYoung, Karen. 2008. "Papers Paint New Portrait of Iraq's Foreign Insurgents." *Washington Post*, January 21, p. A1.

Eckstein, Zvi, and Daniel Tsiddon. 2004. "Macroeconomic Consequences of Terror: Theory and the Case of Israel." *Journal of Monetary Economics* 51: 971–1002.

Fairbrother, Gerry, and Galea, Sandro. 2005. "Terrorism, Mental Health, and September 11: Lessons Learned about Providing Mental Health Services to a Traumatized Population." Century Foundation Report. http://www.tcf.org/Publications/HomelandSecurity/911mentalhealth.pdf.

Falk, Armin, and Josef Zweimüller. 2005. "Unemployment and Right-Wing Extremist Crime." Discussion Paper 4997. London: Center for Economic Policy Research.

Fearon, James, and David Laitin. 2003. "Ethnicity, Insurgency, and Civil War." *American Political Science Review* 97(1): 75–90.

Felter, Joseph, and Brian Fishman. 2007. "Al-Qa'ida's Foreign Fighters in Iraq: A First Look at the Sinjar Records." Harmony Project, Combating Terrorism Center at West Point, December. www.ctc.usma.edu/harmony/pdf/CTCForeignFighter.19.Dec07.pdf.

Fendel, Hillel. 2005. "Saudi Prince: Terrorism Not Caused by Poverty." Israel National News Daily News Service, December 15. http://www.mymarketing.co.il/Print/oX5F1CoC363A07EC2F1BEDA5DFF2BF4AC92B18D517183476B3.htm#a94876.

Fisher, Gordon M. 1992. "The Development and History of the Poverty Thresholds." *Social Security Bulletin* 55(4): 3–14.

Frey, Bruno S., Simon Luechinger, and Alois Stutzer. 2007. "Calculating Tragedy: Assessing the Costs of Terrorism." *Journal of Economic Surveys* 21(1): 1–24.

Friedman, Robert. 1992. *Zealots for Zion: Inside Israel's West Bank Settlement Movement.* New York: Random House.

Gambetta, Diego, and Steffen Hertog. 2006. "Engineers of Jihad." Unpublished paper, University of Oxford.

Gittleman, Jeffrey. 2004. "G.I.'s Padlock Baghdad Paper Accused of Lies." *New York Times,* March 29, p. A1.

Gordon, Michael R. 2006. "U.S. Central Command Charts Sharp Movement of the Civil Conflict in Iraq towards Chaos." *New York Times,* November 1, p. A12.

Gore, Al. 2002. "A Commentary on the War against Terror: Our Larger Tasks." Speech at the Council on Foreign Relations, February 12. http://www.gwu.edu/_action/2004/gore/gore021202t.html.

Green, Donald P., Jack Glaser, and Andrew Rich. 1998. "From Lynching to Gay-Bashing: The Elusive Connection between Economic Conditions and Hate Crime." *Journal of Personality and Social Psychology* 75(1): 82–92.

Green, Donald P., Laurence H. McFalls, and Jennifer K. Smith. 2001. "Hate Crime: An Emergent Research Agenda." *Annual Review of Sociology* 27: 479–504.

Guilmartin, Eugenia. 2004. "Terrorist Attacks and Presidential Approval from 1949–2002." Unpublished manuscript, United States Military Academy.

Hassan, Nasra. 2001. "An Arsenal of Believers." *New Yorker*, November 19, pp. 36–41.

Hester, Jere, and Dave Eisenstadt. 1995. "A Fearsome Car Bomb." *Daily News*, April 20, p. 2.

Hines, James, and Christian Jaramillo. 2004. "The Impact of Large Natural Disasters on National Economies." Mimeo, University of Michigan.

Horwich, George. 2000. "Economic Lessons of the Kobe Earthquake." *Economic Development and Cultural Change* 48(3): 521–42.

Hovland, Carl, and Robert Sears. 1940. "Minor Studies of Aggression: Correlation of Lynchings with Economic Indices." *Journal of Psychology* 9: 301–10.

Hudson, Rex A. 1999. "The Sociology and Psychology of Terrorism: Who Becomes a Terrorist and Why?" Report prepared under interagency agreement by the Federal Research Division, Library of Congress, Washington, D.C. http://www.loc.gov/rr/frd/pdf-files/Soc_Psych_of_Terrorism.pdf.

Hurvitz, Eli. 1998. "The Military Wing of Hizballah: A Social Profile." Masters thesis, School of History, Tel Aviv University, Moshe Dayan Centre for Middle Eastern Studies, Tel Aviv University.

Iannaccone, Laurence R. 2003. "The Market for Martyrs." Presented at the 2004 Meetings of the American Economic Association, San Diego, Calif., January 5.

Iannaccone, Laurence R., and Eli Berman. 2006. "Religious Extremism: The Good, the Bad, and the Deadly." *Public Choice* 128(1): 109–29.

"It's 'More Than Any of Us Can Bear.'" 2001. CBS News, September 11. http://www.cbsnews.com/stories/2001/09/11/archive/main310811.shtml.

Jaeger, David, and Daniele Paserman. 2005. "The Cycle of Violence? An Empirical Analysis of Fatalities in the Palestinian-Israeli Conflict." Discussion Paper 1808. Bonn, Germany: IZA.

Jai, Janet J. 2001. "Getting at the Roots of Terror." *Christian Science*

Monitor, December 10. http://www.csmonitor.com/2001/1210/p7s1-wogi.html.

Jefferson, Philip, and Fred L. Pryor. 1999. "On the Geography of Hate." *Economics Letters* 65(3): 389–95.

Kahneman, Daniel, and Amos Tversky. 1979. "Prospect Theory: An Analysis of Decision under Risk." *Econometrica* 46: 263–91.

Kahneman, Daniel, Alan B. Krueger, David Schkade, Norbert Schwarz, and Arthur Stone. 2006. "Would You Be Happier If You Were Richer? A Focusing Illusion." *Science* 312(5782): 1908–10.

Karolyi, G. Andrew, and Rodolfo Martell. 2005. "Terrorism and the Stock Market." http://fisher.osu.edu/fin/dice/papers/2005/2005-19.pdf.

King, Colbert I. 2005. "Homegrown Hatred." *Washington Post,* July 16, p. A17.

Krongard, H. J. 2004. *Security and Intelligence Oversight: Review of the Department's Patterns of Global Terrorism—2003 Report.* United States Department of State and the Broadcasting Board of Governors, Office of the Inspector General. http://oig.state.gov/documents/organization/41085.pdf.

Krueger, Alan B. 2001. "Gross Domestic Product vs. Gross Domestic Well-Being." *New York Times,* September 20, p. C2.

———. 2003a. "Cash Rewards and Poverty Alone Do Not Explain Terrorism." *New York Times,* May 29, p. C2.

———. 2003b. *Education Matters: Selected Essays by Alan B. Krueger.* Cheltenham, England: Edward Elgar.

———. 2004. "The Impact of Higher Oil Prices." *The New York Times,* May 27, p. C2.

Krueger, Alan B., and David D. Laitin. 2004a. "Faulty Terror Report Card." *Washington Post,* May 17, p. A21.

———. 2004b. "Misunderestimating Terrorism." *Foreign Affairs* 83(5): 8–13.

———. 2007. "*Kto Kogo?*: A Cross-Country Study of the Origins and Targets of Terrorism." Forthcoming in Philip Keefer and Norman Loayza, eds., *Terrorism and Economic Development.* New York: Cambridge University Press.

Krueger, Alan B., and Mikael Lindahl. 2001. "Education for Growth: Why and for Whom?" *Journal of Economic Literature* 39(4): 1101–36.

Krueger, Alan B., and Jitka Malečková. 2003. "Education, Poverty and Terrorism: Is There a Causal Connection?" *Journal of Economic Perspectives* 17(4): 119–44.

Krueger, Alan B., and Jörn-Steffen Pischke. 1997. "A Statistical Analysis of Crime against Foreigners in Unified Germany." *Journal of Human Resources* 32(1): 182–209.

Krugman, Paul. 2004. "Errors on Terror." *New York Times*, June 25, p. A23.

Kunreuther, Howard, and Erwann Michel-Kerjan. 2004. "Policy Watch: Challenges for Terrorism Risk Insurance in the United States." *Journal of Political Economy* 18 (4): 201–14.

———. 2006. "Looking beyond TRIA: A Clinical Examination of Potential Terrorism Loss Sharing." Working Paper 12069. Cambridge, Mass.: National Bureau of Economic Research.

Lebanese Ministry of Social Affairs. 1996. *Population and Housing Survey.* Beirut.

Leonhardt, David. "The Year in Books, 2007." www.nytimes.com/2007/12/19/business/19leonside.html?_r=2&oref=slogin&oref=slogin.

Lerner, Daniel. 1958. *The Passing of Traditional Society.* Glencoe, Ill.: Free Press.

"London Bomber Video Aired on TV." 2005. BBC News, September 2. http://news.bbc.co.uk/1/hi/uk/4206708.stm.

Lynch, Rick. 2005. "Briefing with Major General Rick Lynch, Spokesman, Multinational Force Iraq." Multi-National Force Iraq, Combined Press Information Center, Baghdad, Iraq, October 20. http://www.mnf-iraq.com/Transcripts/051020.htm.

"Madrid Hit by Terrorist Rail Bombs." 2004. *The Australian*, March 12, p. 1.

Malečková, Jitka. 2006. "Terrorists and the Societies from Which They Come." In Jeff Victoroff, ed., *Tangled Roots: Social and Psychological Factors in the Genesis of Terrorism*, pp. 147–61. Washington, D.C.: IOS Press.

Merari, Ariel. 2005. *Suicide Terrorism.* Hoboken, N.J.: John Wiley and Sons.

Mickolus, Edward F., Todd Sandler, Jean M. Murdock, and Peter A. Flemming. 2006. "International Terrorism: Attributes of Terrorist Events, 1968–2004 (ITERATE 3-4)." February 2. http://ssdc.ucsd.edu/ssdc/ite00001.html.

Muslim Council of Britain. 2005. "In the Name of Allah, the All-Merciful, the Most Compassionate." http://www.mcb.org.uk/uploads/Signed_Ulama_statement.pdf.

"Muslim Nations Fail to Define Terrorism." 2002. Associated Press, April 3.

National Commission on Terrorist Attacks upon the United States. 2004. *The 9/11 Commission Report.* http://www.9-11commission.gov/report/911Report.pdf.

Neff, Donald. 1999. "Jewish Terrorists Try to Assassinate Three Palestinian Mayors." *Washington Report on Middle East Affairs,* June, pp. 87–88.

Palestinian Center for Policy and Survey Research. 2001. "Palestinians Support the Ceasefire, Negotiations, and Reconciliation between the Two Peoples but a Majority Oppose Arrests and Believe That Armed Confrontations Have Helped Achieve National Rights." December 19–24. http://www.pcpsr.org/survey/polls/2001/p3a.html.

———. 2006. "Poll Number (22)." December 14–16. http://www.pcpsr.org/survey/polls/2006/p22epdf.pdf.

Palestinian Central Bureau of Statistics. 2002. "Education: Current Main Indicators." http://www.pcbs.org/tnside/selcts.htm.

Pape, Robert. 2003. "The Strategic Logic of Suicide Terrorism." *American Political Science Review* 97(3): 343–61.

———. 2005. *Dying to Win: The Strategic Logic of Suicide Terrorism.* New York: Random House.

Paxson, Christina. 2002. "Comment on Alan Krueger and Jitka Malečková, 'Education, Poverty, and Terrorism: Is There a Causal Connection?'" Research Program in Development Studies, Woodrow Wilson School of Public and International Affairs, Working Paper 207. http://www.wws.princeton.edu/rpds/downloads/paxson_krueger_comment.pdf.

Paz, Reuven. 2005. "Arab Volunteers Killed in Iraq: An Analysis." *Project for the Research of Islamist Movements, Occasional Papers,* 3(1). www.e-prism.org/images/PRISM_no_1_vol_3_-_Arabs_killed_in_Iraq.pdf.

Pew Global Attitudes Project. 2004. "A Year after Iraq War: Mistrust of America in Europe Ever Higher, Muslim Anger Persists." Pew Research Center, March 16. http://pewglobal.org/reports/display.php?PageID=795.

Phillips, Zack. 2007. "Economist Warns against Vague Statements on Security Threats." *Government Executive,* September 13. www .govexec.com/story_page.cfm?articleid=38014&dcn=e_hsw.

Piazza, James A. 2006. "Rooted in Poverty? Terrorism, Poor Economic Development and Social Change." *Terrorism and Political Violence* 18(1): 159–77.

Piehl, Anne M. 1998. "Economic Conditions, Work, and Crime." In Michael Tonry, ed., *Handbook on Crime and Punishment,* pp. 302–19. Oxford, England: Oxford University Press.

"President Addresses Nation." Fort Bragg, North Carolina, June 28, 2005. www.whitehouse.gov/news/releases/2005/06/20050628-7.html.

Raper, Arthur. 1969 [1933]. *The Tragedy of Lynching.* Reprint Series in Criminology, Law Enforcement, and Social Problems 25. Montclair, N.J.: Patterson Smith.

Ricks, Thomas E. 2006. "Military Plays Up Role of Zarqawi." *Washington Post,* April 10, p. A01.

Robbins, Lionel C. 1947. *The Economic Problem in Peace and War: Some Reflections on Objectives and Mechanisms.* London: Macmillan.

Romanov, Dmitri, Asaf Zussman, and Noam Zussman. 2007. "Does Terrorism Demoralize? Evidence from Israel." Unpublished manuscript, Cornell University.

Ropeik, David, and George M. Gray. 2002. *Risk: A Practical Guide to What's Really Safe and What's Really Dangerous in the World around You.* Boston: Houghton Mifflin.

Ruhm, Christopher J. 2000. "Are Recessions Good for Your Health?" *Quarterly Journal of Economics* 115(2): 617–50.

Sageman, Marc. 2004. *Understanding Terror Networks.* Philadelphia: University of Pennsylvania Press.

Sandler, Todd, and Walter Enders. 2006. "Economic Consequences of Terrorism in Developed and Developing Countries: An Overview." Unpublished paper, University of Texas at Dallas.

Schuster, Mark A., Bradley D. Stein, Lisa H. Jaycox, Rebecca L. Collins, Grant N. Marshall, Marc N. Elliott, et al. 2001. "A National Survey of Stress Reactions after the September 11, 2001, Terrorist Attacks." *New England Journal of Medicine* 345(20): 1507–12.

Schwert, G. William. 1985. "A Discussion of CEO Deaths and the Reaction of Stock Prices." *Journal of Accounting and Economics* 7(1–3): 175–78.

Segal, Haggai. 1988. *Dear Brothers: The West Bank Jewish Underground*. New York: Beit-Shamai.

Silver, Roxane Cohen. 2002. "Thinking Critically about Coping with Life's Traumas." G. Stanley Hall Lecture, American Psychological Association Convention, Chicago, August 24.

Silver, Roxane Cohen, E. Alison Holman, Daniel R. McIntosh, Michael Poulin, and Virginia Gil-Rivas. 2002. "Nationwide Longitudinal Study of Psychological Responses to September 11." *Journal of the American Medical Association* 288: 1235–44.

Stecklov, Guy, and Joshua R. Goldstein. 2004. "Terror Attacks Influence Driving Behavior in Israel." *Proceedings of the National Academy of Sciences* 101(40): 14551–56.

Stern, Jessica. 2000. "Pakistan's Jihad Culture." *Foreign Affairs* 79(6): 115–26.

Thompson, J. L. P. 1989. "Deprivation and Political Violence in Northern Ireland, 1922–1985: A Time-Series Analysis." *Journal of Conflict Resolution* 33(4): 676–99.

United States Department of Health and Human Services. 2005. *Terrorism and Other Public Health Emergencies: A Reference Guide for the Media*. Washington, D.C.: U.S. Government Printing Office. http://www.hhs.gov/emergency/mediaguide/PDF/HHSMedisReferenceGuideFinal.pdf.

United States Department of State. 2004. *Patterns of Global Terrorism* (uncorrected version), April. www.state.gov/documents/organization/31912.pdf.

———. 2006. *Country Reports on Terrorism 2005*. Office of the Coordinator for Counterterrorism, April.

Varadarajan, Tunku. 2007. "Milton Friedman @ Rest." *Wall Street Journal*, January 22, p. A15.

Williams, Rowan. 2006. "Benedict and the Future of Europe." Speech at St. Anselmo, Rome, November 21. www.archbishopofcanterbury.org/sermons_speeches/061121.htm.

"World Trade Center Bomb Terrorizes New York." 1993. BBC News, February 26. http://news.bbc.co.uk/onthisday/hi/dates/stories/february/26/newsid_2516000/2516469.stm.

Yunus, Muhammad. 2006. Nobel lecture. http://nobelprize.org/nobel_prizes/peace/laureates/2006/yunus-lecture-en.html.

INDEX

Page numbers followed by *f* indicate figures, those followed by *n* indicate notes, and those followed by *t* indicate tables.

CIA. *See* Central Intelligence Agency
civil liberties: correlation with political
    rights, 78, 82, 100; in home countries
    of terrorists, 7–8, 75, 79, 79*f*, 86,
    92–93, 100; in Iraq, 88–89; measure-
    ment of, 78–79; reducing terrorism
    with guarantees of, 87–89; relationship
    to terrorism, 7–8, 75, 79, 86, 87–89,
    92–93, 100, 148; relationship to eco-
    nomic conditions, 89–90; in target
    countries of terrorists, 79, 79*f*; in
    United States, 88, 148, 154–55
civil wars: definition of, 157; distinction
    from terrorist campaign, 156–57,
    159–61; factors correlated with, 82,
    104; in Iraq, 7, 159–61
Clarke, Richard, 14
Clinton, Bill, 13, 161
Clinton administration, 44
CNN, 134, 135–37
Coca-Cola, 116
Cole, USS, 161
Collier, Paul, 82, 104
Comedy Central, 59
Colombia: attacks on oil pipelines in, 63,
    67; kidnappings in, 67
companies: effects of terrorism on stock
    market values of, 113–18, 115*t*, 116*t*;
    executive kidnappings, 117
crime, relationship to education, 146.
    See also hate crimes

Daily Show, The, 59–61, 65
data on terrorism. *See* terrorism, data on
Davies, Sir Howard, 116*n*
Davis, Darren W., 131
democracy, 82, 87, 88, 117, 129. *See also*
    elections; political rights
deprivation-aggression hypothesis, 16
distance, as barrier to terrorism, 80, 85,
    95, 98–99, 103–4
diurnal pattern of terrorist attacks, 135,
    136*f*

earthquakes, 107, 155
Eckstein, Zvi, 113*n*
economic consequences of natural disas-
    ters, 107, 107–8*n*, 110
economic consequences of terrorism:
    acceleration of existing trends,
    157–58; in Basque region of Spain,

111–13, 112*f*, 113*f*, 119, 155; on com-
    pany stock values, 113–18, 115*t*, 116*t*;
    effects of media coverage, 131–32; on
    foreign direct investment, 110–13,
    162; on growth, 8, 106–7, 111–12,
    112*f*, 157; in Israel, 113*n*; large effects
    of, 8, 108–17, 119; mitigation with
    monetary policy, 155–56; overreac-
    tions, 9, 109; of September 11 attacks,
    106–7, 108, 109, 119, 156, 157–58;
    small effects of, 105–8, 117–19; on
    specific industries, 107, 108, 118, 158;
    spillover effects, 118; stock market
    volatility, 110, 111*f*; uncertainty,
    109–10, 140–41
economic freedom, 87
economic growth, following terrorist
    attacks, 8, 106–7, 111–12, 112*f*, 157.
    See also gross domestic product
*Economic Problem in Peace and War,
    The* (Robbins), 139–40
education, content of, 51, 143, 144–45
education levels: benefits of higher,
    13–14; in home countries of terrorists,
    80, 89; likelihood of voting by, 47,
    146–47; openness to information and,
    147–48; public attitudes toward ter-
    rorism by, 24–25, 25*f*, 27, 27*t*, 28–30,
    29*t*, 31, 45; relationship to crime
    levels, 146; relationship to economic
    growth, 162; relationship to existence
    of hate groups, 17–18; relationship to
    extremist politics, 47, 147; of terror-
    ists, 3, 34*f*, 35, 36, 44, 48, 147–48. *See
    also* literacy rates; terrorism, alleged
    link to poverty and lack of education
Egypt: Iraqi insurgents from, 83, 94, 102,
    103; workers in Iraq, 93–94
Eisenstadt, Dave, 134
elections: effects of terrorism, 129–31;
    participation in, 4, 47, 146–47;
    psychological impact of results of, 159.
    See also democracy
embassies, terrorist attacks on, 66, 72, 118
Enders, Walter, 113*n*
Enron, 110
Erdogan, Recep Tayyip, 13
ETA. *See* Euskadi Ta Askatasuna
Europe, psychological impact of terrorism
    in, 124–26. *See also* Britain; Germany;
    Spain

Romanov, Dmitri, 126
Royal Dutch Shell, 116, 158
Rubinstein, Yona, 109, 127–28, 129
Ruhm, Christopher J., 146
Russell Senate Office Building, 135–37
Russert, Tim, 58–59, 60–61

Sageman, Marc, 39, 44
Sandler, Todd, 67, 113n
Saudi Arabia: civil liberties in, 7, 79; Iraqi insurgents from, 83, 94, 101, 102; terrorist attacks in, 56, 60
Schuster, Mark A., 132
Schwert, G. William, 117
Sears, Robert, 16
Segal, Haggai, 39, 43t
September 11, 2001, attacks: economic effects of, 106–7, 108, 109, 119, 156, 157–58; effectiveness of, 154–55; effects in New York City, 106–7, 108, 119, 157–58; Giuliani's reaction to, 141–42; media coverage of, 132, 134; Palestinian public's perceptions of, 27–28; political responses to, 160; psychological impact of, 119, 120–23, 122f, 124f; television viewing following, 132, 133f; timing of, 135; warnings of, 44
Silver, Roxane Cohen, 120–21, 131
Smith, Jennifer K., 16
social activities of terrorist groups, 151–52
socioeconomic status: public attitudes toward terrorism by, 30–31, 31t; relationship to extremist politics, 47; of terrorists, 3, 33, 34f, 34–35, 39, 40–43t, 44, 45–46, 47–48. *See also* incomes; poverty
Southern Poverty Law Center, 17
Spain: Basque terrorism in, 111–13, 156, 157; economic effects of terrorism in Basque region, 111–13, 112f, 113f, 119, 155; elections, 129; Madrid bombings, 129, 134
State Department, U.S.: attacks on embassies of, 72, 118; inspector general, 65; lack of statistical agency, 64; report on Iraqi insurgency, 84–85. *See also Patterns of Global Terrorism*
state-sponsored terrorism, 14–15n, 145
Stecklov, Guy, 119–20

Stern, Jessica, 13
Stewart, Jon, 59–61, 65
stock market: effects of terrorism on company values, 113–18, 115t, 116t; event studies, 113–17; short sales before terrorist attacks, 116n; volatility in, 110, 111f
Stutzer, Alois, 124–26
Sudan, Iraqi insurgents from, 83, 94, 102, 103
suicide attacks: characteristics of Palestinian suicide bombers, 34f, 34–35; in Iraq, 23–26, 25f, 26f; in Israel, 25, 48; public attitudes toward, 23–26, 25f, 26f; religious affiliations of perpetrators and victims, 72
Syria, Iraqi insurgents from, 83, 93, 94, 102, 103

target countries of terrorists: civil liberties in, 79, 79f; definition of, 67–68; gross domestic product growth of, 75, 79–80; gross domestic product of, 74, 76–78, 78f, 104, 117; home countries as, 71–72; literacy rates in, 75; number of attacks in, 68, 69–70t; occupations of other countries, 81; political effects of terrorism, 129–32; political rights in, 82, 117; populations of, 80, 149; predominant religious affiliation in, 75; relative influence of characteristics of, 66, 72–82, 73–74t, 77t, 90–91
terrorism: analogy to voting, 4, 47, 146–47; biological, 135–37, 138; causes of, 4–5, 7–8; comparison of current situation to World War II, 139–40; costs and benefits of, 161; definitions of, 14–15, 27–28, 54–55, 145–46, 151; demand side, 48–50; diurnal pattern of attacks, 135, 136f; effectiveness of, 153–55, 161; historical factors in, 152; media coverage of, 131–37, 141; number of fatalities, 112–13, 150–51, 157; as occupational choice, 11, 146; political effects of, 129–31, 152–53; public attitudes toward, 23–32, 25f, 26f, 27t, 29t; risk of, 81–82, 129, 138–42, 139t; social context of, 6; state-sponsored, 14–15n, 145; supply side, 47–50; technological change and, 150. *See also* economic